Cock'ood &
An Histc

Cock'ood & The Warren — An Historical View

Edited by
Skip Skerrett & Nigel Stoneman

Published on behalf of the
Cofton Millennium Committee
by

Stormin' Publications

First published 2000

© 2000 Stormin' Publications

All Rights Reserved. No reproduction permitted without prior permission of the publisher

Stormin' Publications
31 Middlewood
Cockwood
EX6 8RN
01626 - 891427

ISBN: 0-9538872-0-0

A CIP catalogue record for this book is available from the British Library

Front Cover photograph of Cockwood Harbour taken by the late John Wilcox who was so much a part of Cockwood village life and reproduced with kind permission of Mrs L. Wilcox

Back Cover photograph shows a spectacular aerial view of Dawlish Warren with Eastdon and Cockwood visible along the shoreline

Typeset in 10pt Garamond
Designed and produced by the publisher in association with The Studio Ltd,
4A Brookside Units, Venny Bridge, Exeter EX4 8JN

Printed in the UK by the litho offset process on 100 gsm Fineblade smooth coated cartridge paper.

Cock'ood & The Warren — An Historical View

Preface	vii
This Yers a Poem 'bout Cock'ood	viii
Chapter 1: Early History	1
St Mary's Church	1
The Old Lime Kiln	2
The Ship Inn	5
The Anchor Inn	5
Cockwood House	8
Eastdon House	10
Cofford Mill	11
Chapter 2: Development of Cockwood	12
Cockwood School	12
Cockwood Chapel	19
The Old Vicarage	19
Cofton Parish Room	20
Chapter 3: Harbour & Estuary	25
The River Exe	25
The Sod	34
Chapter 4: The Coming of the Railway (1840-)	38
Incident One	41
Incident Two	42
The Atmospheric Railway	43
Cockwood Viaduct	44
Exe Bight Pier	44
The Coming of the Tourist. GLORIOUS DEVON !	48
What of the Railway Today ?	50
Chapter 5: Agriculture & Horticulture	52
Violets	55
Pinks	57
Chapter 6: The Warren	58

Chapter 7: The War Years 69

Chapter 8: Clubs & Societies 74
        Dawlish Warren Golf Club 74
        Whist Drive 76
        Cofton Women's Institute 76
        Mothers' Union 79
        Cockwood Boat Club 80
        Cockwood Monday Club 81
        Mother & Toddler Group 82
        Cockwood Cockleshell Mariners 82
        Cofton in Bloom 83

A Short Story: Fact or Fiction ? 84

Acknowledgements 87

Preface

When the Cofton Millennium Committee met to consider ways in which the Millennium should be recognised it was decided to produce a book which would record some of the known history of the area. With this in mind, volunteers started collecting information from local residents and searching in various archives. The result of these labours is presented in the following pages.

It does not claim to be a definitive history of Cockwood and Dawlish Warren. Much of the past history has, of course, been lost or never recorded. It is hoped, though, that the contents will give an outline of the past and some of the developments that have taken place.

Some people might be puzzled by the use of the names Cockwood (pronounced Cock'ood by the native born residents) and Cofton. Coff or Cock appear to have been used at different times for the same stream. However, in 1863 the ecclesiastical parish of Cofton was formed and this embraces Westwood, Middlewood, Cockwood, Eastdon, St Mary's Cottages, and Dawlish Warren. The contents of this book refer to areas within the parish of Cofton.

Of the people who have collected information a special mention must be made of Sally Stoneman and Helen Nicol who have devoted much time to burrowing through old records. John Newberry's wealth of information about Cockwood Harbour and the Exe Estuary has been of great value. The collected information has been prepared for publication by Geoff Drought, Skip Skerrett, Ailsa Spackman, and Alan Willson and their efforts have been invaluable. Nigel Stoneman has done a great deal of work in liaising with The Studio and, without his efforts, it is doubtful if this book would have been produced.

The willingness of local residents to take time to record their knowledge of past events has been greatly appreciated.

Finally, it is hoped that readers will enjoy this account of this particular area of South Devon.

June 2000

THIS YERS A POEM 'BOUT COCK'OOD
by Charlie Bloomfield

There's a village on the River Exe that's knowed by some of 'ee
With a priddy liddle 'arbour called 'Cock'ood'... by the sea
Or Cock'ood on the mud... at least twice a day 'twould be
Carefully watched over by the Boat Fraternity

'Cos 'tis s'posed to be a fishin' place but the catch they makes is tiny
They spends more time in 'Anchor' Bar than out upon the briny
Still with all the paint they chucks about their boats is nice and shiny

There's Bill and Frank and Reg and John and many many more
Some that's rich from Exeter and some down yer that's poor
They sometimes sails out 'under arch' to head for foreign shore
Like Exmouth or the Warren or the Turf Hotel's front door

The place is full of gard'ners too, vurriners most gets the habit
But they don't grow enough good greens to feed a 'arf sized rabbit
Their tools is gwain rusty more work is what they needs
The best thing in their gardens is gurt big clumps of weeds
Their peas 'ave got the maggits and the turmits got the fly
They'd starve to death poor b.......s if it wa'dn't for 'Birds Eye'

Now the summer is a praper time the Grockles gets a tan
They stuffs theirselves with pies and scrump and cockles from our Stan
They shouts and sings "tis just like Heaven'
Down yer with us in glorious Devon

For the old men often tell the tales of the good old days of yore
Of cockle rakin' on the Exe and feudin' on the shore
Who remembers Jimmer, Jacko, Old Tom and Lofty too
Aunt Lil and Farmer Billy for to mention just a few
The family names of Farley, of Dodge and Gilpin too
Helped steer the 'Ship' of Cock'ood and made a 'ansome crew

Of 'Ginny' and of 'Alice' the ladies all in black
With barrows and with cockle rakes filled many and many a sack
And they sent 'em up to 'Lunnon Town' on the Great Western Railway track
It always seems a better place for they that's lookin' back

When the woods was full of Oak and Beech a rustling in the breeze
With Cuckoos in the Spring me lads not rows of Christmas trees
To the days when they had 'Strawberry Fair' around the harbour wall
When the village was for villagers and all of 'em 'walked tall'
For everyone likes Cock'ood some have lived yer all their lives
With all the 'vurriners' thats yer now us 'opes the place survives

ca 1960

CHAPTER 1

EARLY HISTORY

St Mary's Church

In considering the compilation of a parish history to mark the start of a new millennium it seems logical to begin with reference to the oldest building in the parish. As far as is known this is St Mary's Church, with references to it dating back to the 13th century.

One question which has often been asked is why the church was built in its present position, well away from the centre of the village and with few buildings near it. There are many other examples of churches now existing in isolation from any group of houses and, no doubt, there are various reasons for this seeming peculiarity.

In the case of St Mary's it is important to remember that there was a considerable change wrought in the local geography by the building of the railway. Prior to that there had been a broad inlet opening off the Exe estuary, through which the River Coff (sometimes referred to as Cock) ran on its way to join the Exe. There was no Cockwood Bridge and no Cockwood Marsh. Sailing barges came into Cockwood to discharge coal and other products. Clearly there must have been an appreciable depth of water to allow the barges to enter and leave.

Although this inlet narrows by the time Cofton Farm is reached, the present marshy nature of the land near the farm indicates that there was a considerable distance between the firm land on either side. It is clear that there was no place to cross the river (other than by boat) until one reached the vicinity of Cofford Farm. Where the road bridge now spans the river there was a ford across the Coff, part of the track leading from Dawlish to Starcross. Church Road, from Cockwood to Cofton Farm did not exist. There would probably have been, at best, a muddy track along the river foreshore.

Although the early history of Cofton is not recorded it is known that a settlement existed there soon after the Norman Conquest. There were enough inhabitants there to justify building a chapel and it was built on high ground, well above the marshy area. At the request of the inhabitants a permanent vicarage was established in Cofton in 1439.

The church is dedicated to the Blessed Virgin Mary and was mentioned for the first time in a deed of 1270. This deed is lost, but in 1384 Bishop Brantyngham authorised the Vicar of Dawlish to perform divine services at St Mary's. About this time the villagers of Cofton brought an action against John Caynock, the Vicar, to force him to provide a chaplain to serve the chapel of St Mary. (At that time Cofton was known as Cockton or Cokton, the name being derived from the Celtic *cocc* meaning red and Old English *ton* or *tun*, a settlement; in other words 'the settlement on the red soil'.)

At one time John Caynock was pursued by an angry mob to Exeter Cathedral where he had taken sanctuary; they dragged him out and tried to bind and imprison him. For this they were excommunicated. The dispute dragged on for 56 years and ended in 1439 when the parishioners were admonished to attend services and receive sacraments at Dawlish.

Over the next 300 years there were many fluctuations in the life of the church. After 1760 the church was left without a minister and the building fell into ruins.

Many of the stones were carried away for building and repair work and, so the story goes, a neighbouring farmer took the Altar slab to use in his dairy. However, the milk always turned sour and there were so many uncanny noises and unpleasant occurrences that at last the stone was returned to its original home, after which all was well. It supports the present altar. One of the bells — so tradition goes — was carried away by the crew of a Greenland whaler who landed at Topsham and the other was removed by a Mr Rodd who hung it in his home at Doddiscombleigh.

The church remained in this state until William, tenth Earl of Devon, arranged for the rebuilding of the church which re-opened for divine service in January, 1839. The Parish of St Mary's, Cofton was created as a separate entity in 1863. Since then various additions and refurbishments have been carried out. The church plate includes an unusual chalice of mother-of-pearl (given by William Collyn of Kenton in 1839) which is said to be part of the spoils from the Spanish Armada.

The Old Lime Kiln

The Old Lime Kiln is in the garden of a private house, opposite the Ship Inn, and is a listed building. At one time it belonged to the Earl of Devon

Early History

The ruins of St Mary's Church, ca 1832. The image shown is a photograph of the original watercolour, reproduced with the permission of Rosie Kingman.

The altar in more recent times.

The Old Lime Kiln, recently renovated.

Old line drawing with a view of the estuary showing the top of the Lime Kiln in the foreground.

and is believed to be more than 200 years old. Before the railway came barges came up the Exe to deliver limestone, brought from Brixham. There is still a cobble stone path leading from the lime kiln to the river bank, although it is now covered with earth and the main road. Limestone was also brought in by horse and cart from Martock in Somerset. The stone was burnt in the lime kiln in large fires and the lime was then used in the building industry and in agriculture.

The Ship Inn

The building is believed to date from about 1640 and it probably provided refreshment from early times for it contains large old ovens, now exposed, and is believed to be over 350 years old. It was allegedly a well-known smugglers inn with steps leading down to the river whereby brandy and other items from France could be landed. At a later stage it was a victualling house, supplying boats with their needs for sea-going. There were stone slipways leading to the water here and at Middlewood and Westwood.

On the 1840 Tythe Map it is recorded as a house and stable owned by a Mr Jacob Bartlett and occupied by Mr John Ash who was a carpenter. The building was taken on by Charles Coombes some time between 1840 and 1850 and was then run as a Public House, the coming of the railway possibly having an influence on this decision. In 1883 Charles was replaced by Robert Coombes who remained there until at least 1893. Both are buried in Cofton churchyard.

There was a time when women from the village used to bake their Sunday dinners in the huge oven, paying a small sum for each dish. After a time word went around that they were being served with beer at irregular times. The landlord was so angry that he put a stop to the practice.

The Anchor Inn

The earliest known record of the Anchor Inn is on the 1840 Tythe Map when it is recorded as a house and garden in the ownership of Rev. Dr John David Perkins. The land is recorded as being Glebe Terrier land, i.e. land owned by the parish providing income for the Vicar. Dr Perkins was a well-known vicar of Dawlish at that time and also possessed much land and property in Cockwood. The building is several hundred years old and at one time it is believed to have been a Seaman's Mission, possibly when it was owned by Dr Perkins.

Cock'ood & The Warren

The Ship Inn, ca 1960.

Inside The Ship Inn around the same time.

Early History

The Anchor Inn.

In 1844 the Rate Book shows the building as being a pair of houses. The first record of it being a Public House is in 1857 when it was owned by Elizabeth Westcott as a beer and cider seller. In 1870 it was run by Samuel Stokes who had convictions for gaming and out-of-hours sales. In the *Exeter Flying Post* of April 3rd 1872 Hussey and Sons offered for sale by auction "all that freehold Public House called 'The Anchor Inn', situate at Cockwood. This property, from its proximity to the South Devon Railway, where extensive works are now being carried on, offers a desirable opportunity for investment".

The higher ground on which the Anchor Inn stands led to a path towards the railway line, known as 'the batter'. A possible explanation for this name is that, in more turbulent times, it was a location for guns protecting the river mouth.

Cockwood House

Approaching Eastdon from Cockwood there is a section of wall along side the road which bears evidence of being eroded by wave action in the days before the coming of the railway. Cockwood House once stood just inside this wall but the only remaining evidence of the house being there is a pair of granite pillars in the lane leading to Eastdon Farm. Two hundred years ago the driveway to the house led from these pillars.

The earliest surviving reference to the house is an advertisement which offered the house to let at a rent of £8.8s.0d per annum. In the *Exeter Flying Post* of May 16th 1799 the house was offered for sale by auction. From the description of the house in the sale particulars it would seem to have been a Georgian property "with three ground rooms, with pantry and scullery, four lodging rooms, with a closet, also a cellar, with a pound house, stable, ... and a good well of water". In addition there was about a 100 acres of land.

Whether the house was sold at that time is not known but in the early part of the 19th century it was bought by a Dr Joseph Drury. Clearly Dr Drury was a man of substance for he had been a Master at Harrow School for 36 years, 20 of these as Headmaster. He had taught many well-known

---

Facing page. *Map prepared for the Sale of Cockwood House in 1838, following the death of Dr Drury's wife Louisa Drury. It clearly shows the house and vast surrounding grounds (reproduced with the permission of the Earl of Devon and the Devon Records Office, their reference: 1508 M Devon add/E 27/2).*

Early History

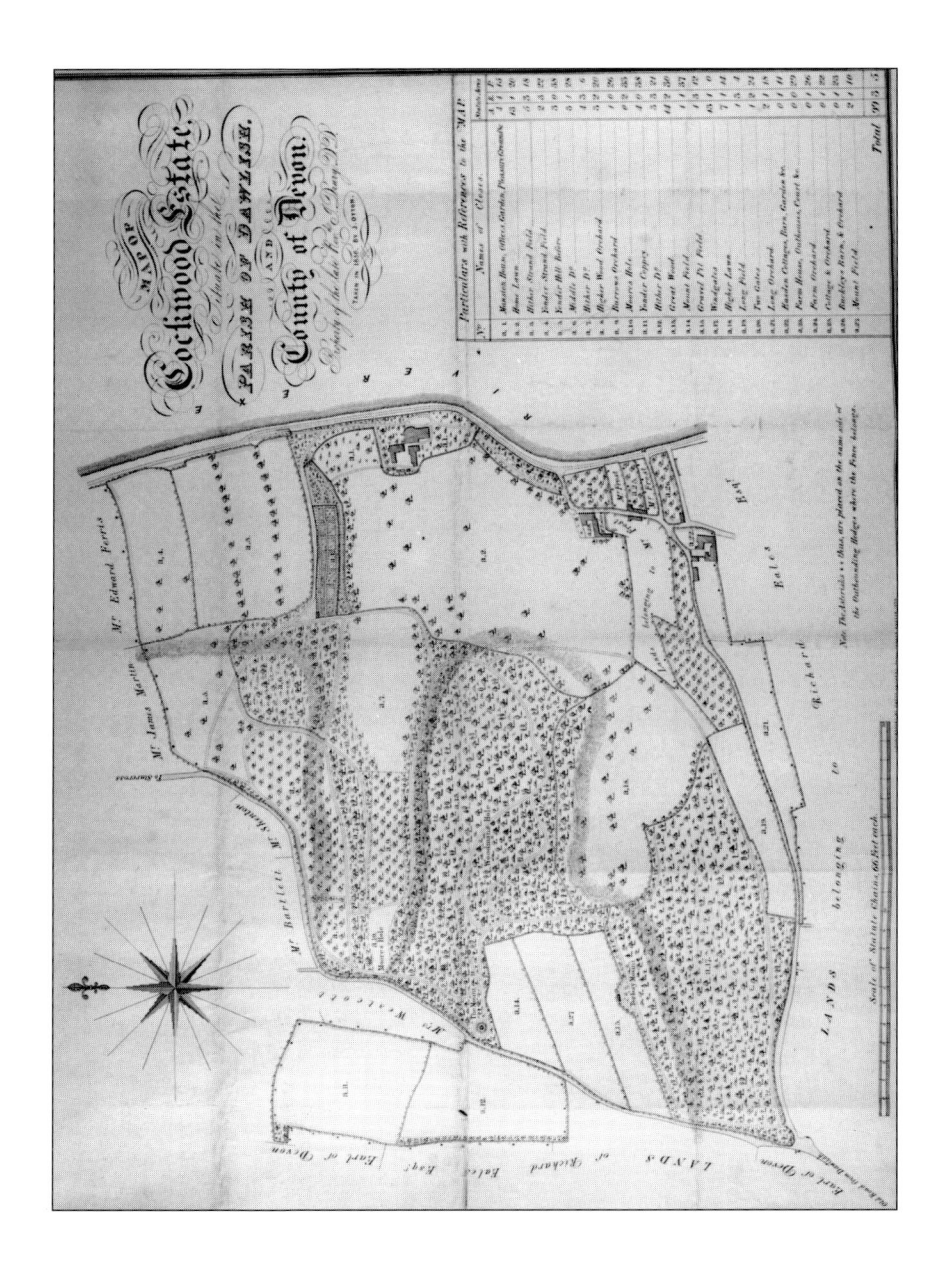

men, including Byron, Lord Palmerston and Sir Robert Peel. When he came to Cockwood he became a magistrate in Dawlish and bought a lot more land in Dawlish and surrounding areas.

Dr Drury died in 1834 and the property was advertised for sale in the *Exeter Flying Post* of January 25th 1838. There is a reference to the house on the Tythe Map of 1840 where the landowner is recorded as The Earl of Devon but it does not appear on any later maps. Presumably the house had ceased to exist, for reasons unknown. With the aid of a dowsing rod Richard Weeks, who farms the land now, has been able to trace the outline of the foundations of the house but, with the exception of the granite pillars, there is no evidence that a fine house once stood there.

Eastdon House

Standing in extensive parkland, the house commands excellent views across the Exe estuary. The early history of the house is not known but the kitchen, servant's hall and cellars suggest that part of it was built in the 16th century with the bulk of the present house being built at a later date.

The earliest known reference is of the Eales family living there in the latter part of the 18th century. This was clearly a family of substance for Richard Eales (born 1759), was Lord of the Manor of Dawlish and Clerk of the Peace for the County of Devon, reputedly for 50 years. There are memorial tablets to members of the family in Cofton Church, one to Charles Eales who was Principal Clerk of Committees in the House of Commons in the 19th century. In addition, there are memorial tablets in Starcross Church as well as a number of graves in the churchyard.

The name lives on in the form of Eales Dock, located just before Dawlish Sands holiday camp in Dawlish Warren. The dock was built before the railway came and before the road was built so that there would have been easy access from Eastdon House.

The house was bought in 1905 by J. G. D. Partridge, although the house was occupied by the Waterfield family from 1900-1910. The Partridge family lived there until the 1980s and continued to use Eales Dock for all of that time. In 1885 Anna Partridge paid for the erection of the porch for St Mary's Church in memory of William Partridge. In 1905 J. G. D. Partridge was married in Ireland but as an expression of thanks for his marriage, he paid for the erection of the lych gate at St Mary's.

Access to Eastdon House was via Shutterton Lane which swung around and ran in front of the house. In the early part of the 20th century the then owners decided that they did not wish this to continue and so they gave a piece of land to allow a new section of road to be built to link the road to the Warren. This was on condition that the existing road was closed. This was duly done and following this the houses in Shutterton Lane were built. Remnants of the old road can still be seen at the backs of the gardens of these houses.

On top of a high bank just past Cofton Country towards the main road can be seen what is known as Cofton Cross. A modern cross set up by the Earl of Devon early in the 19th century when St Mary's Church was rebuilt. It is said to replace an ancient cross.

Cofford Mill

Across the main road just past Cofton Cross and further past Cofford Farm, along the track to Duckaller is the site where once stood a cornmill, known as Cofford Mill. This was once part of Cofford Farm and there are records of this mill dating back to the 16th century. Very little is known about this mill, it is unclear whether it was operated by water or whether it was horse-drawn. Maps show it to have existed until the early 1900s but as to why it disappeared there is no known record.

CHAPTER 2

DEVELOPMENT OF COCKWOOD

Cockwood School

The school opened its doors for the first time on 30th September 1872. Thirty two children were admitted and were required to bring their penny fees. Two years later Dawlish School Board took it over and the roll increased into the fifties. By November 1875 the numbers had reached sixty five. A supplementary teacher was appointed for the infants and the teaching of sewing. Monitress assistants had been employed and were to continue for many years.

During these early years, prior to compulsory attendance imposed in 1888, absences were frequent. Children were needed to help with gleaning and fruit picking and there were many holidays for local events such as Regattas, Fair Days, Flower Shows and Races. Such absences were smiled on but late coming was discouraged. Canings were frequent and as many as ten children were caned on one morning in May 1875 for being late for school. Corporal punishment was a regular feature of school life and the aptly named Mr Henry Bircham who was master of the school from 1876 to 1878 used it frequently, despite the strong opposition of parents. In November 1876 he notes in the log book "Cautioned three boys who came to school with their hair too long". Times have not changed that much.

It is difficult to realise how little concern there was about childrens' health and welfare in those days. Epidemics came and went and the diseases named are factually recorded without comment. Measles, lung infection, pneumonia, chicken pox, scarlet fever, anaemia of the brain, whooping cough and influenza are all mentioned regularly and typhoid is reported on two occasions. During outbreaks the school was occasionally closed, sometimes for long periods; at other times attendance was cut to fifty percent.

The Medical Officer of Health (MOH) first came to visit the school on the 19th December 1901. His second visit was a year later when he came to say that relatives of children absent with chicken pox should attend school. A

Development

School group, 1883.
From the back, left to right: Mr Ruth, Reggie Lightfoot, Bill Andrews, Jack Doyle, George Brooks, Jack Hoare, George Shepherd, Jack James, Joe Wright.
Frank Gee, Joe Wight, Farmer Hills, Fred Back, Bill Murch, Day Dodge, Clara Harris.
Alice Stokes, Eva Knowles, Maud Hutchings, Alice Tarr, Maud Hoare, Alice Farley, Ada Lintern, Emily Wight, Lucy Murch, Lena Back.
Jessie Ellis, Flora Wills, Bertha Hutchings, ?,?,?, Stokes, Charlie Coombes,?.

change of policy brings about an enquiry from the MOH in January 1905 about a case of measles in the village; on 4th April that year he tells the Headmaster that brothers and sisters of children with measles are to be excused. However, that epidemic continued to spread despite the Doctor's new concern. His visits from then on became more frequent but it is not until 5th June 1913 that a school nurse appears, six years after the start of the School Health Service.

It was a long time before a break during school hours was considered desirable but eventually on 6th July 1894 "In order to fulfill Article 12(E) there will be an interval of ten minutes for recreation at both meetings of the school, viz. from 10.40-10.50 am and 3.15-3.25 pm".

In 1905 the MOH took particulars of childrens' paid employment after school hours, which shows some concern for their welfare. A further

13

School group, 1911.

School group, 1915.

Development

improvement saw the emergence of School Dentists and the first recorded visit was made in 1916.

On 30th November 1942 school dinners were introduced. The Headteacher commented shortly afterwards "The children look much improved in health, probably due to the school dinners provided". School dinners have continued and now give children choice of dishes or the opportunity to bring their own sandwiches. Cockwood has been extremely fortunate with kitchen staff and the standard of cooking is always excellent.

In the early days the health of the staff was not much better than that of the children. Two of the assistants employed were chronic absentees due to illness, one of the many monitresses developed a gastric ulcer as did a young assistant teacher later on. However, Mr Ruth, Headmaster for forty years from April 1878 to March 1918 was able to teach throughout his time with very few absences. During that period he survived epidemics, flood, fire and tempest. And he met them all. He records flood after heavy rain, fire when he was called from school to his home where the adjoining house was alight and on one very stormy occasion in 1877 he logs "Gale damage to the thatch roof".

When it started the school had just one main room. Four years later a second room was added for the infants. Now there are three classrooms on a very restricted site and inevitably the play area is below the recommended level. In November 1877 mention is made of a pump being in working order in the playground. Its function was "to assist in the cleanliness and tidiness of the children". The pump has long since disappeared but children still refer to "the Pump House" when an extension of the classroom building to provide a store brought the open pump under cover. Refurbishment of the premises in 1892 probably included much needed extra toilet facilities as, at the start, the school had only two toilets, one for the boys and one for the girls; and when one of them was out of order, the children (over sixty of them!) all used the one facility.

In 1902 and again in 1903 HM Inspectors recommended the provision of an additional classroom but nothing was done for many years. The school was redecorated in the summer of 1919 and the holidays were extended to eight weeks. The yard was tarred and sanded in 1936. The kitchen was added in March 1953. Then in October 1968, sixty six years after the first recommendation, a new infant room was built. Since then there have been many minor improvements made to the classrooms.

Inevitably history has touched Cockwood School over the years, whether through great national events or socio-economic changes in the area.

Thus there were holidays for:

21st June 1887	Queen Victoria's Golden Jubilee
6th July 1893	Wedding of Duke of York and Princess Mary
	Children invited to Belvedere at Powderham by the Earl of Devon
21st June 1897	Queen Victoria's Diamond Jubilee — whole week
23rd May 1900	Relief of Mafeking
7th March 1902	The King passed through Cofton and Dawlish on his way to Dartmouth and Plymouth
2nd June 1902	End of South African War
6/7th May 1935	King George V and Queen Mary's Silver Jubilee
6th November 1935	Wedding of the Duke of Kent and Princess Marina
21st January 1936	School closed for King's funeral
7th May 1945	VE Day
20th November 1947	Wedding of Princess Elizabeth
17th November 1948	Birth of Prince Charles
13th February 1952	Prayers said for King George VI and the new Queen. Children listened to the proclamation on the radio
29th May–2nd June 1953	Weeks holiday for Coronation of Queen Elizabeth II
26th February 1960	Marriage of Princess Margaret
1st July 1969	Investiture of Prince of Wales seen by Class 1 on TV at invitation of Mrs Sime of Dawlish

Although many of the entries in the school log book over the years are routine there are some interesting and even amusing events recorded.

Fees were often very hard to collect: "27th March 1878 - £1.2s.3d irrecoverable arrears cancelled by School Board" In 1887 "... left this school to attend Starcross School because the fee there is 1d" and "Punished ... for writing indecent expressions on his slate"

In 1911 there was a most remarkable heatwave. The Headmaster records 29th/30th May 74°F in main room; 7th July 76°F in main room and 12th July 80°F in main room and 122°F outside.

During the first part of the Great War Cockwood children made their small contribution when, at the suggestion of the Education Committee, they went collecting chestnuts. A couple of months later these were sent off to the Director of Propellant Supplies, London. An obscure source of fuel perhaps? Their contribution during 1918 was much greater however. The Education Committee then sponsored blackberry picking and fourteen half days were devoted to the task. The amounts picked ranged from 52 lb to $114\frac{1}{2}$ lb and a staggering total of $1,268\frac{1}{4}$ lb were gathered over a period of five weeks.

22nd June 1923 — on Thursday afternoon ten children were absent, their parents considering the roads unsafe because of motorcars taking people to and from Starcross to vote.

4th May 1926 — a laconic entry records "Owing to strike I have been unable to reach school until 9.50 in the morning" (Headteacher).

Regulations are introduced in February 1932 concerning the transfer of children at 11 years of age to "schools organised for Senior Scholars" and again in July 1933 concerning the admission of children "no scholars under the age of five years of age are to be admitted to this school".

The duties of the governors seemed to be many and various. On 26th May 1948 we find, "I asked Mr Yorke, a governor of the school, to inspect the pudding which was sent for the children's dinner as I considered it to be unpalatable; this he confirmed". The same Mr Yorke takes twelve boys with children from Dawlish Junior School in his boat out to HMS Agincourt, anchored in the bay, to be conducted over the vessel.

On 29th April 1953 a group of boys aged twelve to eighteen years trespassed on school property and damage was done to the roof and various windows. Encouragingly on the 26th May "the Police Constable has given me 22s.6d which he has collected from the boys who damaged the roof and windows — 10s.6d has still to be paid by one who admitted to breaking a pane of glass" Oh, for the days!

By 1973 the School had 101 children in it. A class was operating in the parish room, not a very suitable teaching environment.

Two years later Nesta Thomas was appointed as the school's first Deputy Headteacher. By the summer term of 1977, Gordon Baird, The Headteacher, became ill and was obliged to take early retirement. Dennis Careless took over the school for a year until a permanent replacement could be appointed. September 1978 saw Rod Crook became Headteacher, having moved from a Deputy Headship in Cheshire.

During the next 10 years the cycle of school life continued much as before, though the Education Authority decided to restrict pupil entry to ensure the school returned to three classes. The School did have a much needed upgrading of the toilet facilities — rebuilding ensured that the children could go to the toilet inside. However, the slate screen and the pump house were thus consigned to history. Shortly afterwards, interior re-modelling changed the shape of two classrooms and gave the school more usable space.

Aerial shot of Cockwood School, ca 1960.

The dawn of a new age began when a sponsored walk was held to raise money to by a ZX81 computer for the school. The school has come a long way since that early beginning. Residential trips to Wembworthy were started and have remained a feature of school life ever since.

The end of the 1980s saw major changes in the world of education which were to have a huge impact on the school. The advent of Local Management meant that the school could take responsibility for a delegated budget and, for the first time ever could decide how to spend it. This was to lead to an improved staffing pupil ratio and a huge increase in the amount of money spent on books and equipment. An office computer ensured that the school was able to manage the budget.

Another building project saw the office being changed into a library and resource area, a small extension to classroom two and the construction of a new office at the front of the school.

Some of the notable achievements by Cockwood pupils in recent years have included David Hodge passing GCSE Mathematics at the age of 10 and becoming a regular member of the English Schools Chess Teams, Kris Davis playing cricket for the Devon under 11 team, and the school Kwik Cricket team representing Devon. Despite the rather limited facilities the school has done remarkably well in a wide range of sporting events.

The last few years have seen another series of educational changes. Children are now tested at the ages of 7 and 11 in English, Mathematics and Science, and the school has to set annual targets for improvement. In 1998 the school had its' first Ofsted Inspection. This was successful and led to classification as a "very good school". In 1999 the school, received an honourable mention in the Chief Inspector of School's Annual Report, and Rod Crook was invited to Highgrove House to meet Prince Charles.

There is no doubt that the school has played a major part in the life of the community and residents are rightly proud of what has become the best, albeit one of the smaller primary schools in Devon.

Cockwood Chapel

It is recorded that the preaching of the Gospel, which led to the creation of Cockwood Chapel, started in a cottage in Middlewood on 25th April 1885. The venue was later changed to a corrugated iron building on Cofton Hill.

The witness flourished, numbers increased and land was donated next door to the Village shop and the local brethren built the present chapel which opened for services on 1st October 1910. From that day to the present there has been an ongoing witness in the form of Gospel preaching, Bible teaching, women's meetings and Sunday School.

The Old Vicarage

St Mary's Cofton was created as a separate parish in 1863 and shortly afterwards it was agreed that it was desirable to have a Parsonage in order that the incumbent could reside in the midst of his parishioners.

The Earl of Devon gave the site (value £100) and the Ecclesiastical Commissioners made a grant of £1000. However, a document of 1865 asserts that 'the peculiar circumstances of the district and the deficiency of building materials (particularly of stones, which will have to be brought by water from Babbacombe), will necessitate a much larger outlay than is usual in such cases.'

An appeal was made, therefore, for a sum of £400 in addition to the grant by the Ecclesiastical Commissioners, to carry out the work. It was recognised that 'the district of Cofton is occupied mostly by agricultural

A recent photograph of The Old Vicarage.

labourers, and there are no resident landowners; hence the necessity of appealing to persons residing beyond the district.'

Lord Devon, in addition to having the church restored, paying for the school to be built and giving the site for the new Parsonage had endowed the living with £100 per annum. He now gave a further £100 in response to the appeal; W. Cosens Esq. gave £25 and W. Gibbs £10. Presumably the rest of the money was raised, for there is a note that the parsonage was completed in 1867. However, one piece of correspondence dating from 1884 survives and in this the vicar appeared to be querying whether the Earl of Devon had paid the amount that he had agreed to give. Unfortunately the outcome is not recorded.

The Parsonage continued to be occupied by the Vicars of Cofton until 1987 when it was sold by order of the Diocese of Exeter against the wishes of the parishioners.

Cofton Parish Room

The idea of a parish room was first mooted in 1885. On November 2nd six persons — the Vicar, two churchwardens, the Earl of Devon and two others — signed a declaration stating that they considered themselves trustees of a trust formed to acquire a site for the parish room.

A bazaar was held and raised £94. This was to be used, together with any other monies that were added, for the purchase of a site. It took about seven years to find a piece of land that was suitable and it was bought with donations from relatives of the then Vicar, Rev. C. P. Benthall. This is the land on which the parish room now stands.

The building was erected in 1893-4 at a cost of £307, including fencing and gates. A further £57 was spent on buying furniture, games, books, etc. Other items of furniture were given or lent. By September 1894 enough money had been raised to pay the final instalment to the builders and to complete the payments for furniture.

The trust deed stated that the room could be used for Vestry or other meetings for the Parish of Cofton, Church Sunday School, Night school or reading room, Mothers' meetings, and 'generally for such purposes as will tend to the benefit, advantage and well-being of the parishioners of Cofton, but that the room shall not be used for any religious services other than of or in connection with the Church of England.'

In 1893 the Cofton Men's Club was formed with the object of 'promoting the moral, social and intellectual welfare of the members. The proceedings of the undenominational and non-political.' The subscription was 10s.6d per year and the club was open daily, except Sundays, from 7-10 pm. One of the rules was that 'lads under 18 may not smoke in the room.'

The responsibility for running the hall passed from the trustees to Cofton Parochial Church Council in 1965. In 1985 representatives from various organisations in the village were invited to join the Parish Room Committee and the day-to-day responsibility for the management of the parish room is now discharged by this committee.

A 1937 procession past what is now The Village Stores in honour of the coronation of King George VI.

1993 procession of Cockwood schoolchildren with the aid of Street Heat, an Exeter-based musical group. They marched to a samba rhythm from the school down Cofton Hill for the Village Fete of that year.

Two pictures showing the demise of Highbury, 5 Cofton Hill in April 1986. Part of the cob wall at the end of the house simply collapsed. Fortunately the then owner, Mr Reg Russell, was away at the time. The property was repaired but is now some 2.5 metres shorter as can be seen when comparing old and recent photographs.

BROAD GAUGE EXPRESS NEAR STARCROSS, G.W.R., ABOUT 1890.

Broad Gauge Express, ca 1880, with "Greystones" in the background.

A modern "Sprinter" train on the same piece of line.

24

CHAPTER 3

HARBOUR & ESTUARY

The River Exe

Before the advent of the railway Cockwood ranked as one of the minor ports on the estuary. Vessels carrying coal and stone and other cargoes discharged their loads at or near Cockwood. The Port of Exeter was concerned lest Cockwood should provide a cheaper port facility and thereby reduce the traffic to Exeter. In the 18th century there were also salt works at Powderham, Cockwood and Dawlish Warren. In 1844 The South Devon Railway was constructed along the western bank of the Exe, effectively sealing off what was previously known as Cockwood Lake.

Cockles, mussels and oysters were obtained from the estuary. In December 1885 20 people who had cockle and mussel bed fishing rights were prosecuted for damaging the oyster beds and were fined £1.

Another interesting aspect concerning cockles relates to a lady known as "Cockle Mary". A local resident, she was a cockle raker and she scratched her living from the River Exe at the start of the 20th century. Leaving her barrow at the slipway and taking her rake and basket, she started at the cockle steps on the Warren Road. Raking with the tide she would fill quart tins and bury them, marking their positions with white sticks. As soon as the tide turned she would gather her tins and return to her barrow. This was her routine for 6 days of the week, but on Saturdays she would load up her weeks harvest of cockles and, with the help of a porter, would take the train to Exeter St Thomas Station, selling her cockles at 4 d a quart. It must have been a hard life, working through all sorts of weather and with limited protective clothing.

In her book entitled *The Estuary of the Exe*, published in 1902, Beatrice Cresswell refers to an interesting tradition concerning Cockwood. She admitted that she could not find "chapter and verse" for it, but it was claimed that the manorial rights for the foreshore in this area belonged not to Kenton, as one would suppose, but to Cofton. This arose it was said, owing to a shipwreck on the shore, when the people of Cofton extended

Cock'ood & The Warren

'Cockle Mary' at work raking the estuary mud for the fruits of the sea.

A lovely old picture showing activity around the harbour. The Anchor Inn can be clearly seen in the background but no sign of the parish room yet to be constructed.

themselves to rescue the crew of the vessel, while the good folk of Kenton looked on. It is possible that the latter have been maligned for Cofton is certainly within easier reach of the shores of the Exe than Kenton. Be that as it may, the coveted "rights" of the foreshore were bestowed upon Cofton as a reward.

In the late 1900s "Strawberry Fair" was then an annual event, held on the nearest Sunday to the end of June on which the tide was high about teatime. Baskets of strawberries were spread out along the harbour wall and visitors came from far and wide, some from Exmouth in rowing boats, to eat as many strawberries as they could for a nominal sum, washed down with large quantities of cider. In these days anyone who had travelled more than three miles could be served with drinks at any time of day, even on Sundays. The Anchor Inn on the waterfront did a roaring trade and literally rolled out the barrels!

Although strawberries are still grown in the area the custom of the annual fair has died out and for many years in it's place the 'Cockwood Revels' was held annually. These were held at the highest evening tide of the summer. All the events, organised by the local boat club, took place in the water, or in the mud! Once again the wall was crowded with people who came from near and far to watch the fun, and the Anchor Inn still did a roaring trade, but there were no strawberries to go with the cider.

When we view the river today we see a vast area of water with sailing boats, cruisers, water skiers and sail boarders. The Exe has become a playground to be enjoyed by all those who are happy to take part in water sports. The Exe, in the Cofton area, is bordered by 'The Warren', which makes it a very protected area from the sea. Although shallow in many places it gives a vast waterway that can be used by the many differing activities.

However this is how we see it today. If we look back into the history of the Exe we can see a totally different picture. The Exe estuary created during the glacial period is quite unique in its formation. Near the mouth of the estuary the river broadens to almost one and half miles wide. At the entry to the sea, at low tide, the water is only six feet deep and the entrance quite narrow. When viewed at high tide, from the Warren, the river Exe takes on the appearance of a vast six-mile long inland lake.

Moving down the valley the waters widen out creating marshy areas along the route. Ideal for wild fowl and other forms of wildlife.

Navigational channels in the river, created by the flow of the water, are narrow and shallow but being tidal the depth can vary considerably according to the tidal cycle. Large boats moving up the river were obliged

Cock'ood & The Warren

Cockwood harbour viewed from the railway bridge.

A more recent picture with considerably more boats at their moorings.

28

to seek the assistance of pilots as the channels were very difficult to follow and bore no relation to the shape of the river banks. Many boats were too large to proceed far upstream and moored at Topsham and the cargoes were unloaded onto smaller boats, which could enter the Port of Exeter.

The minor ports of Exmouth, Starcross, Lympstone and Cockwood were allowed to unload boats carrying stone for the lime kilns and coal. Many of these cargoes would then proceed to their destination by horse drawn trucks. Timber carrying boats were frequently moored off our coast awaiting the tide to take them into Exeter.

The many restrictions of the river made a significant difference to the type and size of craft able to enter the waters. Large vessels had to wait for the spring tides to be able to enter and exit through the narrow entrance. However the protection given by the Warren from a stormy sea led to the waters becoming known as a bad weather haven. Commercial traffic in the Exe wishing to enter the ports of Exeter or Topsham frequently had to moor in the river adjacent to our shore to await a high tide that would allow further passage upstream. Records show that on one occasion at least thirty freight carrying boats were moored across the river and each was able to swing free on its anchors without fear of colliding. This does lead one to speculate that maybe the area has changed over the many years with silting up of many of the channels. Surprisingly the number and size of the boats gradually increased, colliers being the largest, one of 252 tons entered and left the Exe. At one time as many as 33 lighters were plying up and down the Exe assisting the unloading and loading of the larger vessels.

Cargoes carried in and out of the Exe appear to cover almost every commodity that could have been needed for the running of a busy city. It must be remembered that the railway was not built and running until the mid-1800s. Roads were poor with only horse drawn vehicles and carriages. Nearly every commodity that could be carried by a boat was shipped to the heart of Devon via Exeter, all these boats passing through or mooring close to Cofton.

One of the most important commodities that the Exe became famous for was wool. Exeter from early times was a flourishing market for wool, which was eventually exported all over the world. A study of Exeter shows the many wealthy merchants working in the wool trade developed the city. This trade ran for many centuries long before other commercial activities started to take off. During the seventeenth century the trade in wool and woollen products reached its peak. Tiverton and Exeter being the centres of the trade, each using the ports of the Exe to transport the exports throughout the world. The trade, based mainly on the serge weave which was used for almost all requirements from military uniforms to high quality outfits, according to the standard and finesse of the weave gave this area an almost monopoly of woollen products. For almost five hundred years Devon's wool was traded and bartered throughout the world but in the late 1700s this started to come to an end. Italy, Spain and Holland, Devon's largest customers started to produce their own cloths. Britain was at war in many theatres throughout the world and found it difficult to maintain exports. By 1817 the trade was as good as finished with the woollen products produced in this area supplied only to the trade in the British Isles.

Throughout the centuries most of the trade handled within the Exe was conducted on the east bank, where the waters have proved to be deeper and the natural channels more favourable. Topsham and Lympstone became the most significant ports within the estuary and in their hey day had boat building yards capable of making 'Men of War' during the Napoleonic period, and fishing boats which regularly travelled to the Newfoundland fisheries. Boats were fitted out and supplied with all that was needed to visit Greenland and the whale fishing fields. Two whale fishing vessels were known as the *Exeter* and the *Lympstone*. Records kept from 1755 to 1787 show that whalebone, fins and oil brought back from the fisheries was traded in the Exeter market. Today all that remains of the whale-fishing era is an area of the river known as Greenland.

Surprisingly Exmouth hardly existed throughout the whole of the period when trade was at its highest. It only became a port during the mid-part of the nineteenth century. Prior to this it was a small hamlet, which due to its pleasant climate, became a fashionable watering hole for the gentry. Unloading of cargoes for Exmouth took place on the beach or at Topsham. Rope makers and sail makers established themselves during the mid-1800s together with other subsidiary trades for shipping. Gradually the largest fishing fleet in Devon located themselves in Exmouth with 58 boats operating during the peak. The construction of the railway to the new docks between 1865 and 1868 ensured that Exmouth became the main port of the Exe with rapid loading and unloading and transportation to the major markets throughout the country.

Gradually trade from the ports of the Exe began to dwindle. The emergence of the railway and road transport ensured that goods could be moved more quickly to the ports capable of taking much larger vessels. Timber and coal were amongst the last of the commodities to be carried up the Exe and into Exeter. The last boat of any significance using the Exe and travelling down the river and by our shores was the famous sewage boat owned and operated by South West Water. This came to an end in 1999 when the European laws stopped the dumping of waste in the Channel waters.

The largest boats that we will now see are the Cruisers from Exmouth and Torquay taking tourists on tours up the river to the Turf Inn or to see the rich wildlife that is now returning to these waters.

During the early 1920s the local population awoke to find the Sod full of logs. A freighter had unloaded its cargo of cut logs (each the size of a telegraph pole) and had them floated into the harbour. It is not entirely clear how these were eventually removed.

In December 1943 the Cardiff steamship *South Coaster*, which was bound for Exmouth docks with a load of coal, went aground on the Pole Sands and broke her back. She was eventually refloated and ultimately beached in the shallows within the estuary, close to the railway line that runs along to the Warren. She was partially scrapped where she lay, but her mast and hull still show at low water.

1974 saw the harbour totally frozen over. Ice floes were everywhere. A local informant assures us that this happens on a regular thirty-year cycle. So 2004 *should* see us all freezing up again. The River Exe was in an even more precarious state. Ice floes half a mile long and several feet thick were moving up and down the river with the tide, frozen in the ice were marker poles and portions of landing stages. The floes moved up and down destroying everything in their path. All navigation and mooring buoys were ripped from their moorings.

No boats dared to venture into the water, as they would have been cut to ribbons. Tyres were hurriedly attached to boats to try to protect the hull but even these were cut to pieces by the ice. Water birds were seen on the floes with their feet frozen into the ice.

In the early 1950s the local population awoke to see what appeared to be a suicide. Hanging from the mast of the wreck of the *South Coaster*, was a body dressed in ladies clothing. The police were inundated with telephone calls informing them of the tragedy. On arrival the police commandeered local boats and these were rowed out to the wreck with a view to rescuing the body, ambulances were standing by to assist. After struggling with the tide and the difficulties of gaining access to a very difficult part of the wreck the police found that the body hanging from the mast was nothing more than a cleverly disguised tailor's dummy. With

Cock'ood & The Warren

The frozen waters of the estuary near Starcross Pier in the big freeze of 1974.

disgust and their reputation slightly dented the police left the scene and the dummy was left hanging from the mast. Over a period the weather gradually played its part and stripped the dummy of its clothing. Eventually the dummy disappeared. The 'Wag' responsible for this prank is probably still resident in the area but has not been identified.

Oliver Jackson was born and brought up in the area in the early years of the 20th century and was very much at home on the river. He recalls that on one occasion a seaplane landed in the river. Oliver rowed out to it and the crew asked him if he would take them to Exmouth. Oliver agreed and, at their request, he went to collect them again at 11 pm. It would be interesting to speculate what might happen if a seaplane landed in the estuary under the present conditions. No doubt there would be a flurry of activity on behalf of police, coastguards, HM Customs and sundry other agents.

Also, our local Honorary Harbour Bosun, John Newberry has been involved in two rescues of visitors who rather foolishly got themselves into difficulties. On the first occasion John and a friend were collecting winkles on Bull Hill Sands when they noticed a group of Chinese tourists had walked out from Exmouth onto the sands. Already the tide was on the flow and the sands were rapidly becoming covered. John approached the Chinese visitors and told them to leave quickly as they would soon become cut off as the water was rising quite rapidly. The only reaction was smiles all round and total incomprehension. No matter what John or his friend said the visitors just smiled back. Suddenly they became aware of their predicament and the mood changed to one of fear. Fortunately for the visitors John and his friend had arrived on the sands each in his own boat so they were able to put the visitors into the boats.

However the boats were overladen, therefore rowing out of difficulty was not a choice and they were unable to get in themselves. The water by now was rising very quickly and John and his friend were up to their waists. All they could do was to steady the boats by wading through the water and pushing them into the shallowest part that they could find. With a stroke of luck the Exmouth pleasure boat appeared and they were able to attract its attention. The boats were pushed to the side of the cruiser who took the Chinese on board and to safety.

On another occasion, early one morning in 1998 John was on duty at the harbour's edge. The weather was poor and the forecast was for a bad day and not one for a day out in a small boat. Voices could suddenly be heard and sounded as if they were coming from outside of the harbour. These

Cock'ood & The Warren

gradually became more strident with shouts for help. On reaching the embankment a small upturned boat could be seen out in the estuary with four people hanging on rather desperately. Without any thought for his own safety in the choppy water John rowed the boat club dinghy out and managed to get the four safely aboard and then returned to the shore.

Another feature of the harbour is that for some years, a pair of swans made their nest in the muds on a raft that floats up and down with the tide. This raft was made by a local birdwatcher who noticed that the nest kept on getting washed away each spring tide.

The Sod

For a stretch of water to be entitled the Sod gives no clue to the reality. This very unglamorous and rather deriding name has come about over the years by what appears to be default. Fortunately our many visitors will never hear this name used. They will always refer to their visit to Cockwood Harbour. Even if they did see only the mud!

It is unlikely that anyone will be able to put an exact date on the first use of a footpath that was constructed from the north shore to the south shore

The final section of the railway bridge being lifted into place.

of Cockwood Lake. Before this the inhabitants had to walk or ride on horse back to the west of the village, almost as far as the Church, to find a suitable crossing over the marshy area. This is probably now where we see the signed footpath close to Cofton Farm. Even this can, during the winter months, become impassable.

The footpath would have been constructed well before the days of the railway and must have been subjected to the vagaries of the weather and the tide flowing into the lake. No doubt there were many times when repairs would have been necessary and the local inhabitants recruited to repair the damage.

Why 'The Sod', the footway could just as easily have been called the turf or the clod. If reference is made to the dictionary the definition of a sod is ... a rectangular piece of turf... Just imagine how many of these 'sods' had to be cut and then carried to the site and laid to make a footpath. Only to be washed away on the next spring tide. Maybe after experiencing the many repairs to the footpath, the name was given by the local inhabitants and 'it' gradually became lost over the years.

For many years the roadway over the water linking the Starcross road to Cockwood was known as 'The Causeway'. This would seem to be a very appropriate name, but for some unknown reason the name has become lost and has now been substituted with the name 'Cockwood Bridge'. This new name seems to have little character and belies the origins and efforts that must have been undertaken by our forbears to build and create an interesting structure, albeit infuriating when caravans and coaches are vying with each other to cross in different directions. Such activities however give great amusement to the diners at the Anchor Inn who can watch the antics of the drivers becoming very frustrated in the hold-ups. We at least all know how to avoid this situation if it arises.

The harbour, now known locally as the Sod, has seen many events and happenings. The coming of the railway changed the whole character of the area and eventually became one of the causes for the demise of the lime kiln. The type of craft using the water has changed from barges, to sail and then to boats with engines and sails or engines only.

Motorbikes have ended up in the water after trying to take the bend in the road too fast. Many cars have ended their days in the harbour trying to take the corner from the Warren road too fast. On one occasion a car careered around the corner hit the low wall and ended up on top of and collapsing a moored boat. The boat owner managed to claim, through his insurance, a new craft, which was a little surprising, as the sunken boat

View across to Southbrook from the tow path on the Cockwood side of the harbour. Ilex House is clearly visible just right of centre.

Ilex House.

was far from seaworthy. Late one night a car driven far too fast ended up in the Sod, local residents rushed to help out the driver, who to their surprise ran off as fast as he could go. Then to everyone's surprise the car mysteriously disappeared even before the police arrived. One or two locals know the mystery of the disappearing car but they are not talking. One very embarrassed chauffeur, was travelling back from Dawlish late one evening, when he mistook the slipway, outside Ilex House, for the roadway and ended up on the foreshore. It would be interesting to know exactly what his employer, seated in comfort in the rear seat of his Daimler had to say. A Mini travelling along the Warren road clipped the wall of the harbour and ended up on its side in the mud. Patrons of the 'Anchor' rushed to help and waded into the mud. To their amazement the side door, now facing upwards, opened up and a man, described as the size of a mountain, started to disentangle himself. The helpers found it hard to believe that a man of such a size could ever have got himself into the Mini. The straight road from Starcross has always been a temptation for speedsters, needless to say, a car raced down this stretch, failed to notice the bend went ahead into the lay by and over the bank into the Sod. Fortunately all the accidents have ended up without any serious injuries. We all hope it remains that way.

Many contests have taken place in the mud, with welly throwing and tugs of war. Each ensuring that the participants end up totally covered from head to foot in the rich river 'Coff' mud.

CHAPTER 4

THE COMING OF THE RAILWAY (1840–)

Standing on the northern shore of Cockwood Lake a small group of Engineers and Surveyors were trying to decide the route for a new railway. The residents of Plymouth had started to bring pressure on the Government of the day to be connected to the fast improving railway network being established throughout Britain. Connections to London were desperately needed to help with local trade and commerce.

Many routes were explored and then discarded for one reason or another. Attempts were made to avoid the land around the Earl of Devon's estate at Powderham but to no avail. Consideration was given to routing the line behind the hamlets of Kenton, Starcross and Dawlish but each of the valleys ran at right angles to the coast and then ended in the hills making a route very difficult to establish. The coastal route seemed to be the best but this meant that the water at Cockwood Lake and the marshes at Eastdon had to be crossed. All of these problems could be solved but at a considerable expense.

The leader of the surveying group was a young engineer who was rapidly making a name for himself in many areas of engineering and building. Isambard Kingdom Brunel, not an easy man to work with, very egotistical and history shows that he had a short temper and demanded total loyalty from those working with him. Councils and Companies that employed Brunel had to suffer his difficult manner. Despite his failings he had a brilliant mind and was regarded as the finest engineer of the day and one that during his short lifetime made many outstanding engineering masterpieces.

A route was eventually agreed upon, which was very close to what we now see today. The newly formed Exeter, Plymouth and Devonport Railway Company submitted their plans for approval. However they were doomed to failure, as the company was unable to raise the necessary funds to build the railway and the company foundered.

1842 saw the revival of interest in the railway with the larger companies of The Bristol and Exeter Railway, The Great Western Railway and the Bristol and Gloucester Railway all providing finance. Together they formed a company called The South Devon Railway and plans were submitted to parliament for approval. Significantly at this stage The Earl of Devon became a shareholder in the company and he was appointed as a director, a part that he played actively throughout construction of the new railway. The newly formed company retained the services of Isambard Kingdom Brunel to oversee the whole project, which he had estimated, would take a maximum of three years to complete.

At this stage it must be identified that the land within the Cofton Boundary was quite wild and under developed, no significant roads existed and marshes spread from the hamlet of Cockwood down to 'The Warren', an inhospitable stretch of sand dunes which was largely wasteland and unusable. A basic golf course had been established and a rifle range for army volunteer recruits to use for practice firing. Today we know this area as 'Dawlish Warren' but the title Dawlish was only added at a much later stage when the area became popular with tourists and the railway needed a name to identify the area.

The hamlet of Cockwood consisted of only a few houses and no Inns existed. The main commerce of the area was the Old Lime Kiln, which we see today as ruins, and farming.

The building of the railway commenced with the embankment bordering the Powderham estate taking shape quite quickly. The line from Exeter through Exminster, Kenton and Starcross was constructed with little difficulty. However the problems started when the engineers reached Cockwood. The Earl of Devon had requested and been granted the right of way for a Carriage and Horses to be able to access the shore of the Exe at all times. This meant the construction of a stone archway at the northern end of Cockwood Lake. The picture on p. 40 shows the eventual construction, one that is still in existence today.

The contractor for the structure of the viaduct came upon many difficulties but mainly the depth of the mud. Pile driving, on a previously unexpected level took place, the wooden piles having to be driven to a depth of 30 feet before any form of foundation could be established. Wrought iron had to be used to join the timbers, an expense that was unplanned, the number of arches had to be increased to gain strength. The picture and the records seem to be in conflict here as they vary by one archway, but the picture gives a very good impression of how the initial viaduct would have appeared.

Cock'ood & The Warren

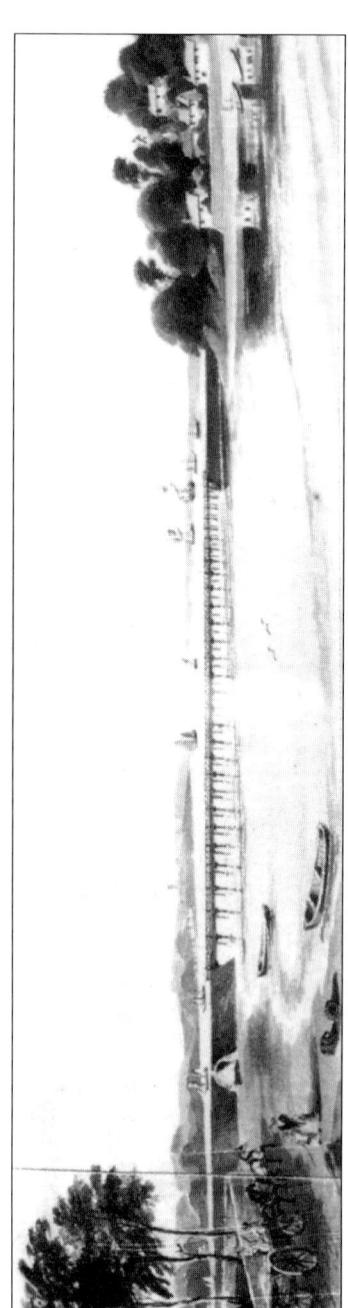

Cockwood Lake showing the viaduct spanning the water. The "Earl of Devon's arch" can be seen on the far left.

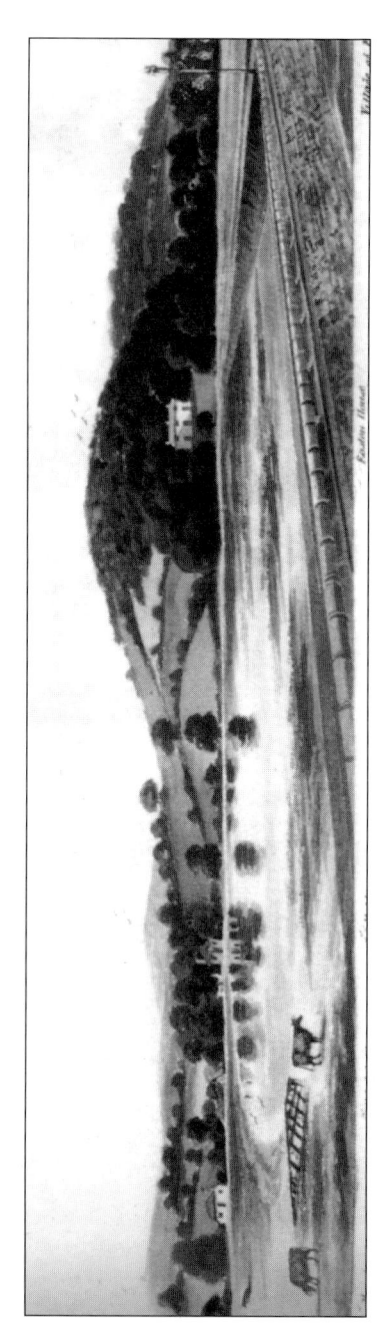

Shutterton Lake with Eastdon House in the background. The picture shows the embankment that was constructed to take the railway through the marshy land and the 'atmospheric' tubes can be seen running between the lines.

Coming of the Railway

Incident One

The building of the railway brought many additional craftsmen and labourers to the area. This meant that they had to be accommodated as near to the site as possible and food and the inevitable drink had to be on hand. An Inn was established on the northern shore of Cockwood Lake called the Half Moon, beside this, cottages were built to accommodate the workers. This site is now Cockwood Garage, just to the west of the Old Lime Kiln.

It is recorded that on the night of 19th December 1844, a Mr Richard Brock, a respectable yeoman, who resided at Botchell Farm, Dawlish, had a drink at the Half Moon. Also in the Inn were four navigators, as they were called, or labourers working on the railway, all of whom had been drinking. Mr Brock left the Inn and was followed shortly by two of the labourers. The Inn Landlord being suspicious also followed with another unnamed man, each was armed, one with a poker and the other with a stick. They passed the two labourers who were returning to the Inn. Shortly they came upon Mr Brock who had been assaulted and bruised. The record states that it was one o'clock on Sunday morning and Mr Brock had had stolen from his

Half Moon Garage, ca 1930, then owned by the Guest Brothers. Now known, of course, as Cockwood Garage.

possession, a silver watch, 5 half sovereigns, 6 half crowns and three shillings. The constable from Starcross was contacted and he eventually tracked down the labourers to an address in Exeter, where they were apprehended. Unfortunately no record is made of their eventual sentence.

Incident Two

The building of the viaduct spanning Cockwood Lake took a great deal more time than was anticipated due to the problems previously explained. This meant that the railway line up to the viaduct was completed and steam engines could bring materials right up to the working site to try and hasten the construction.

The contractor building the viaduct was treating all the timber with tar as a preservative. A normal procedure when placing timber in salt water. However they must have been very generous with the quantity used as it is recorded that an engine moving on to the incomplete viaduct dropped some hot coals and the tar ignited. The engine then travelled at top speed to Exeter and returned in what is described as the most remarkable time with a 'Fire Tender' on board to tackle the blaze. Workmen in the mean time had collected water from The 'Courtenay Arms', Starcross and extinguished the fire. It is also recorded that no serious damage was inflicted on the viaduct. The timbers must have been very strong indeed.

The construction of the railway line between Exeter and Teignmouth continued as quickly as the terrain permitted, the project now being well behind schedule. Brunel had always intended to open the line with atmospherically operated engines (this item is covered in a later paragraph). As the problems with the atmospheric operation had not been solved, pressure was now being brought upon him to get the line open with the use of conventional steam engines. Several dates were set but not met. Teignmouth on one occasion had a carnival arranged to meet the first train, which did not arrive.

Eventually a date was set for Saturday 30th May 1846. Many dignitaries arrived in Exeter for the opening; the steam train was all prepared and ready to leave. Brunel himself was nowhere to be seen. At a few minutes to midday he arrived and went straight to the train and it left for Teignmouth with a great fanfare. No one had informed Teignmouth of the occasion and it arrived with little interest from the residents of the town. Turning the engine around it then returned to Exeter. **The railway had arrived!**

The Atmospheric Railway

The residents of south Devon nicknamed the project as 'The Atmospheric Caper' as will be seen in this section.

Brunel had been studying a new form of propulsion for a railway that had been patented by two brothers, Jacob and Joseph Samuda, some years earlier. The system was operated by a pipe being pumped free of atmosphere to create a vacuum. Into the pipe a sealed valve was inserted and this was sucked along by the vacuum. This form of propulsion had some extremely good advantages.

1. Very fast smooth acceleration.
2. High speeds could be attained, up to 70 mph.
3. The smooth operation gave additional comfort to passengers.
4. Cheaper running costs over conventional steam engines.
5. Ability to operate on steep gradients where steam engines found difficulty.

The Samuda brothers had quite successfully built atmospheric railways in West London, Dublin and Croydon, all of which seemed to be running well, although not for a long, testing period.

An Atmospheric Railway needed many pumping houses and a considerable amount of pipe laying. This took a long time to achieve, and as it was an unproven system in a sea air environment, problems occurred that were totally unexpected.

After several false starts, and subsequent improvements being installed,

A typical pump house. The Atmospheric pipes abutting the lines can be clearly seen.

the Atmospheric Railway started on Wednesday 23rd February 1848. The railway started to run into problems almost straightaway. No one had foreseen that the leather sealed atmospheric pipe would give trouble in a salty atmosphere. The corrosion on the pipes and the leather drying out and cracking failed to maintain a seal to the required vacuum.

Frustration had now set in at the continual delays and additional expenditure. The backers of the scheme withdrew any further finance for the project and it ceased to operate after the last run of the day on Sunday 10th September 1848. The Atmospheric Railway had operated for a period of only seven months.

The atmospheric engines were sold for very little money; the coaches were converted and used as standard rolling stock. The atmospheric pipes were lifted and sold for scrap value. The pumping stations, with few exceptions, were dismantled. Conventional steam engines were brought back onto the line.

Cockwood Viaduct

In 1896 it became necessary to start the replacement of the wood constructed viaduct. The engineers of the day designed a three iron span viaduct on stone embankments. The work commenced to build the stone embankments. Again the depth of the mud caused many problems. Vast quantities of stone were needed to create the foundations before it could be faced with cut stone. A source of local stone for the foundations was found just to the south of the viaduct. This was quarried and made into the causeway as we see it today. The local quarry can still be seen. It now stands back from the railway as Kenbury Crescent, Cockwood. The stone facing for the embankment was brought to the site from Torbay quarries by the use of large barges being towed up the Exe.

When completed the viaduct had three spans or openings to the River Exe. At a later stage one of the openings was removed. This item is covered in the section on the 'Cockwood Boat Club'.

Exe Bight Pier

Proposals to build a pier from the embankment south of Cockwood started as early as 1863. The intention of the Exe Bight Oyster and Fishery and Pier Company was to create two ventures. The first primary role was to create a large oyster bed between the proposed new railway embankment, the new

Coming of the Railway

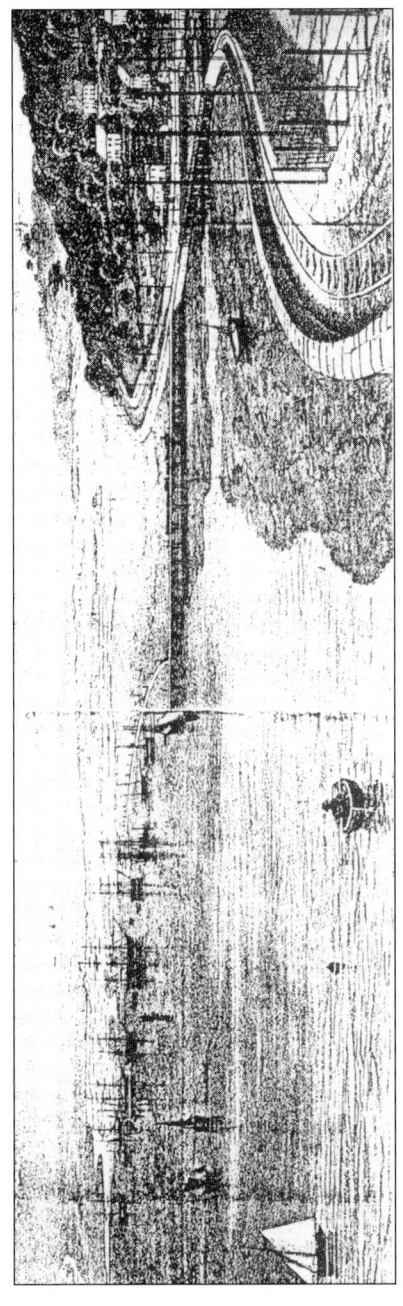

An artists impression of the pier and bight with Cockwood Viaduct and harbour to the left. Significant artistic license is in evidence but nevertheless a wonderful picture.

45

pier and the Warren. Oysters were at a premium price during this period due to their popularity with the upper classes. The second role was to have a pier giving access at all times to the deep water of the Exe.

Opposition to the project came from all directions. The local dredging of mussels was threatened within three miles of the pier. Exeter Corporation was concerned that the trade through the Exeter canal would be affected and tried to impose many court orders against the pier. Exe mariners saw the pier as a danger to shipping. All these oppositions failed but each one cost the newly formed company large fees in legal expenses.

Work eventually started in March 1867. However the site had been moved further to the north than originally planned.

This fact was not noticed by the authorities and the construction of a longer pier became necessary. The reason for this is not entirely clear. A siding with a rail track was constructed parallel to the embankment and the track ran the full length of the pier.

The pier opened to commercial traffic in January 1869 and there is evidence that considerable quantities of coal was unloaded from freighters. Records show that coal was transported from the pier to Exeter merchants and to the Exeter gas works.

The Pier Company ran into problems from the start. The oyster beds were flooded when a severe storm on 31st January 1869 breached the outer warren. The Exeter canal was taking traffic into the heart of Exeter. Exmouth docks had been in the course of construction, throughout the period of wrangling, and were now able to take traffic at any time. Money for the operation of the pier had always been short and no more was forthcoming. Customs facilities had never been established on the pier so foreign cargo ships were unable to discharge goods.

By the summer of 1871 it became clear that the Company could not survive and it went into liquidation. The pier was offered to the Corporation of Exeter who declined the ownership. Eventually the pier was handed to the Earl of Devon and the few remaining shareholders were paid a final dividend of 5 farthings in the pound. The pier continued to be used as there are records that show that the Vessel *Victoria* discharged a cargo of coal in 1874 for delivery to Exeter, Teignmouth and Newton Abbot. Trade, as limited as it was, appears from the records to have ceased by 1878 as the sidings were deleted from the railway working timetables. By 1888 the pier had been finally dismantled, with the stumps of the siding piles remaining to this day, as a reminder of the unsuccessful attempt to establish a port at Cockwood.

Coming of the Railway

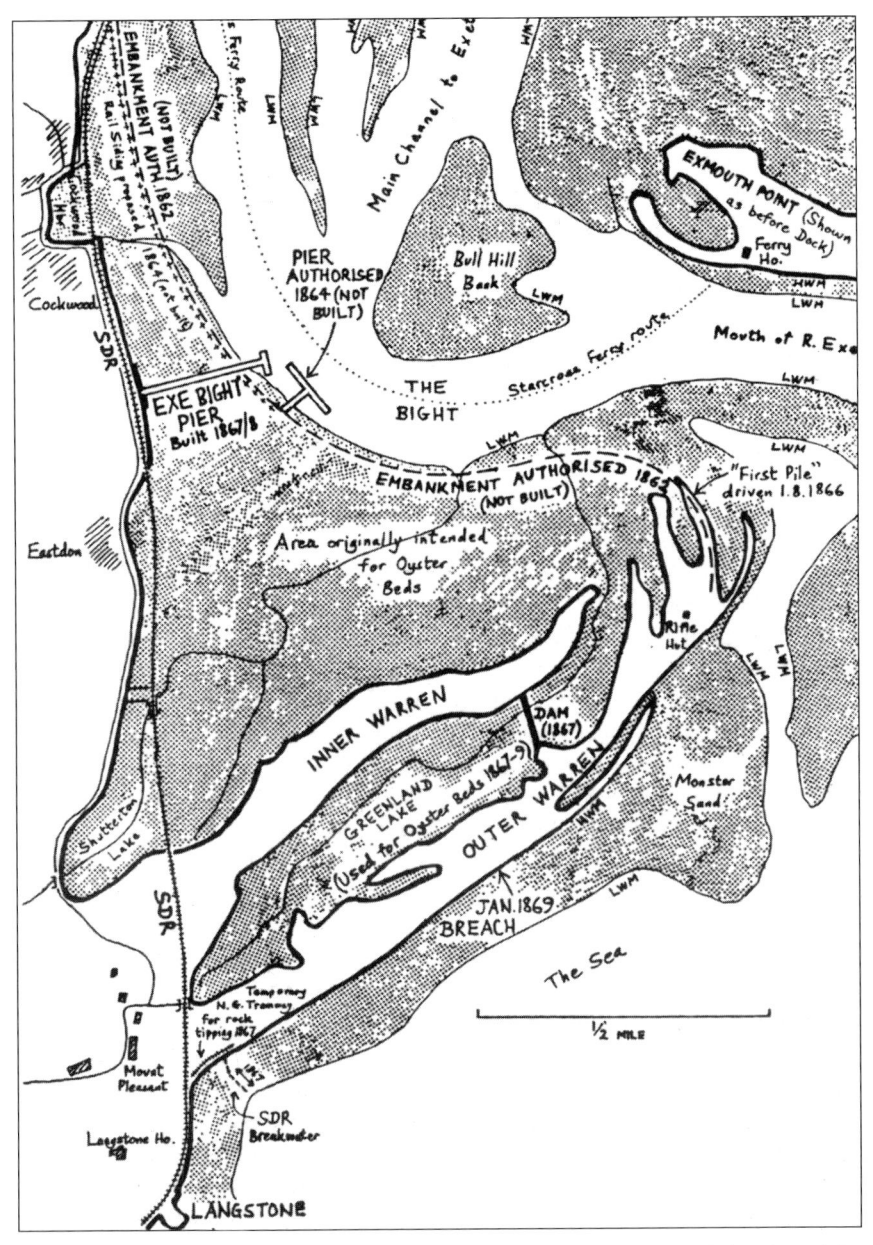

The plan shows the original site of the shorter proposed pier and the site of the longer pier that was eventually built within the estuary.

The Coming of the Tourist. GLORIOUS DEVON !

The south coast of Devon during the early 1800s had become the playground of the wealthy. Those with the means to use horses and carriages travelled to the seaside for the invigorating air. Swimming was not regarded as a sport at this time and was virtually unknown. As we move into the latter part of the century and the advent of the car small communities encouraged holidaymakers but this again was amongst those able to purchase and run an expensive motor vehicle. Dawlish became known as a resort and small family run guest houses appeared.

The railway changed everything and opened up the area to all. The first records show Sunday School outings being organised to the seaside. Trains would run from Bristol through all the towns en route picking up passengers and extra coaches. When the train arrived it was far too long for the short platform and had to pull forward and stop many times to allow the passengers to alight and enjoy the seaside at Dawlish and Teignmouth. Hotels opened on the seafronts and the seaside holiday was established.

Bathing in the sea at this time became popular, although it had to be carefully controlled and segregated. Bathing stations were built for people to visit and change into swimwear. Beaches were for one sex only. Men and Boys were not allowed to mix with Women and Girls. The famous Bathing Machines came into use for those with a little more money. These were wooden constructions, similar to a caravan, into which Ladies would disappear to change into their swimwear. Strong men would then push the bathing machine into the water and retire quickly. The ladies were then at liberty to enter the water by a short ladder. Complete discretion at all times.

The demand for good beaches soon found that amongst the best available was an area called the 'Warren'. The railway for once was very quick to see the opportunity and in 1905 opened a small station. It was given the name 'Dawlish Warren' to identify it from Dawlish town and the name is now here to stay. The station opened direct onto the sands and the public had a short walk over the dunes to the beaches. The area became very popular for the day-tripper and soon enterprising merchants opened tea tents for refreshments. Large numbers came from mid-Devon and Somerset to visit the newly opened beaches of Devon.

The Warren with its large area of wasteland appeared to be an ideal place to site sidings for the use of the farmers with agricultural produce and livestock to be sent to markets. By 1912 the sidings had been built and

Coming of the Railway

Warren Halt, ca 1905.

Dawlish Warren Station ablaze. Was it wise to build a wooden construction in the days of steam trains, or should the youngsters in the foreground be brought in for questioning?

49

were in use, livestock pens were available together with large sheds to store the farming produce. Records show that one of our own smallholders, Oliver Jackson, produced flowers and strawberries, which were shipped to market via the Dawlish Warren sidings.

Sadly the sidings never flourished, the reasons are not entirely known, maybe it was due to difficult access to the area and they eventually ceased to operate in early 1930s.

The sidings remained empty for some time until the Railway Board brought in 'Camping Coaches' for the use of its employees. These we see on site today. Many have been refurbished and give comfortable living accommodation to the holidaymakers.

The Holidaymakers flocked to the Warren in the 1930s and soon local farmers started to let small pitches for tents to be erected for overnight sleeping. Camping became very popular during the Glorious Devon summer. 1939 saw the end of the holiday making for Dawlish Warren as the beaches became fortified to prevent the enemy making a possible landing. The whole of the area became a fortified site to repel any possible invasion. Today it is almost impossible to see any of the fortifications built.

Soon after the end of the war in 1945 the defences were removed and the seashore freed of the mines that had been buried within the sand.

The sands were once again open to the public. Holiday weeks became an established way of life and the Warren as popular as ever. During the early 1950s the sites used for tents started to take caravans. The public started to demand more than just beaches and swimming for their holiday stay and the Holiday Camp came into being.

Larger companies bought up the sites and expanded their operations adjacent to the shore. Permanent static caravans came onto the sites and the public just had to arrive to enjoy the wonderful Devon holiday experience.

What of the Railway Today ?

On holiday weekends there are numerous trains carrying the holiday-makers arriving from many parts of the country, including Wales and Scotland. Being diesel-hauled, sadly, the new locomotives are made in Canada and Spain, the coaches in Belgium, not Swindon, Doncaster, Crewe or Eastleigh. The owners are no longer just G.W.R. or Southern Railway.

If you see a gathering of people near the local railway track, you may get a reminder of past decades, when the steam engine was supreme, with the

Coming of the Railway

Great Western steam train travelling across the now defunct middle arch.

chocolate and cream of the G.W.R. then the customary livery of the coaches.

Just occasionally, the Steam Engine is 'King' once more in Devon.

Mr Brunel would have been pleased.

CHAPTER 5

AGRICULTURE & HORTICULTURE

As with most other parts of the country there have been vast changes in the use of the land of this area. Many small farms existed in the early part of the 20th century but amalgamations have taken place so that there are fewer but larger farms. Small herds of milking cows were commonplace and as recently as the 1970s one such existed at Cofton Farm.

Now there are no milking herds or beef cattle being raised in the area. Flocks of sheep do exist but most land is devoted to arable cultivation, with the harsh, alien yellow flowers of rape crops making an unwelcome intrusion into the spring landscape. And, of course the other significant change in the use of the land since the Second World War has been the

Cofton Farm at the time of its sale in 1950. Note St Mary's Church in the background.

Agriculture & Horticulture

Eastdon Farm, ca 1950.

rapid development of the holiday and tourist industry which offers better financial returns than agriculture.

In the 1920s Cofton became very agricultural with many market gardeners and fruit growers, some of whom had worked on the Mamhead-Starcross Timbercamp Railway, which finished about 1922. (The rail line followed the present Mamhead road and joined the siding at Starcross.)

An interesting insight into the way of life in the early years of the 20th century is given by Mrs Inez Beck in the following paragraphs in which she describes life on a smallholding at Eastdon

> "The Hamlet of Eastdon, consisted of a few thatched cottages, a farm and a farm house, and fields planted with a variety of crops. There were no laboursaving devices available to us in those days. There was no running water from a tap, just a pump, and the privvy was in the garden. All the cooking was done on a kitchen range, and the flat iron was heated on the top; sometimes this got rather smutty. There was a copper in the outhouse for washing clothes. Hot water for the house was kept in a bath near the fire. Lighting was supplied by oil lamps and lanterns.
>
> Work on the ground was done manually and by horses. After the day's work, the horses had to be fed and watered and settled down for

the night in a bed of straw. When the high tide brought in the seaweed, this was gathered, by hand (sometimes at night) and spread on the fields and ploughed in. This acted as a splendid fertiliser. All produce was planted and picked by hand and taken to the shops or market with horse drawn wagon. Some produce was sent to London on the special train which went from Starcross station every evening.

Violets were a speciality in this area. Bunching them was a tedious job, as they had to be counted individually and kept damp until they were boxed and sent off to London. In those days the flowers were large and wonderfully scented. On a wet day the lanes smelled sweetly of violets.

Gradually things changed. Some of the old sheds were taken down and a few lean-to greenhouses were put up along the wall. Cucumbers and tomatoes were grown in these. Gradually the work was done by a crawler tractor and the horses disappeared. The life of the market gardener was arduous. It was not a nine to five job but continuous; wife and family all joined in to help. With no refrigeration available, crops had to be harvested at exactly the right moment. All things considered it was a hard life but a good one".

In the 1930s and 1940s Cofton in springtime was very beautiful with gardens covered in plum and apple blossom. It was a very productive area with 25-30 men employed. Local towns were supplied with many tons of plums, apples, damsons, gooseberries, raspberries and strawberries in many varieties, many now only a memory. Some years there would have been as many as 30 tons of plums with varieties including *Dittisham* and *Orange* plums.

The *Dittisham* plum is so named from the Dittisham Valley, leading to the River Dart, where the plums grew in abundance. The fruit, normally picked by the first and second weeks of August, is not unlike the roundish *Victoria*, red in colour and juicy. It is not classified as a dessert flavour but is nevertheless very tasty and makes jam and preserves of great quality and colour. There are still some 50 trees in the grounds of the Old Lime Kiln, with a few others in Cockwood.

Transport for these products, plus untold tons of vegetables and new potatoes, to local shops in Dawlish, Teignmouth, Shaldon, and Torquay was usually by about eight 35 cwt lorries or vans in the 1930s. There were a few more vans in the 1940s as flower growing increased for the London Market.

Agriculture & Horticulture

Strawberry picking, ca 1960.

On one occasion when Princess Margaret was scheduled to open the extension to the Royal Naval Memorial on Plymouth Hoe there was difficulty in obtaining strawberries for the banquet which was to follow. A Torquay wholesaler was unable to procure any in that area but eventually contacted Oliver Jackson who was able to supply the fruit as he specialised in growing early strawberries.

Violets

The *Viola odorata* or sweet violet, was one of the first flowering plants to be grown commercially, being sold in the markets in Athens around 400 B.C. The most famous violet seller was Eliza Dolittle written about by the author George Bernard Shaw. Other authors who were also inspired by the violet were Shakespeare and Tennyson who wrote poems about their fragrance and charm. In Devon, however, violets were grown only for local demand, but in 1891 two brothers named Westcott, who grew violets at Cockwood, sent a few bunches by train to London and found that the returns were greater than obtained locally.

The first Violet farm was established at Dawlish in 1916 and many other holdings sprang up in the area. By 1926 the number of British violets reaching the market at least equalled those from France, aided partly by a Government tariff on imported flowers. Steady expansion continued until 1930 when a boom in violet growing took place with a 500 per cent increase in the Dawlish area by 1936.

The old tangled clumps that we now see in the woodlands about the villages bear no resemblance to the superb specimens that could be produced with a little care and attention. It is probably the most superb flower to respond to good management and attention.

Mrs Grace Zambra was a noted authority on violets. In 1932 her book *Violets for the Garden* was published and gave guidance for the growing of specimen violets. An enlarged and beautifully illustrated edition was published in 1938.

After the First World War smallholdings were established on the Exeter Road and in Port Road to provide opportunities for returning ex-serviceman to make a start in horticulture. In practice, it seems that not many men took up this offer and the holdings eventually came into the hands of commercial growers. One of these was A. G. Lammas who set up a violet farm on the Exeter Road.

Violet growing was a labour intensive business which could be profitable as a family-run business but not so easily achieved if labour

The site of Lammas Violet farm on the main A379 Exeter–Dawlish road before St Mary's Cottages.

had to be employed. Lammas attempted to diversify by selling "Devon Violets" perfumes and scents, in addition to bunches of flowers. Today it is probable that the firm would have run foul of the Trades Description Act for it is alleged that the essence was imported from France.

During the Second World War the acreages permitted for violet growing were severely restricted and did not fully recover after the war. Another factor that hastened the decline of violet growing was the introduction of the *Harrick* variety, grown in Cornwall. This was a much larger flower than the *Princess of Wales*, although not possessing such a rich scent as the latter. Eventually Lammas sold up and soon after violet growing ceased on that site.

In 1948 Col Oliver Jackson and his wife Anne came to live at Little Orchard at the top of Cofton Hill. They worked the adjacent land, growing flowers and fruit. Oliver negotiated with Munroes, a well-known firm in Covent Garden, to transport flowers such as lilies, pinks, anemones, and gladioli. Munroes were keen to trade with small businesses from the South West. Truckloads of flowers departed most days for Covent Garden from Starcross. Transporting fruit proved less successful due to damage during the long journey.

Pinks

In recent years there has been a development of the growing and marketing of pinks. Cecil Wyatt, although badly disabled by polio, succeeded in producing a new race of hardy, sturdy plants suitable for both garden and cutting. John Whetman and Sons of Houndspool, Dawlish, continue the work of development and have contributed greatly towards the raising of disease-free pinks. Now grown under glass, great quantities of the flowers are marketed locally as well as being sent to the London market.

CHAPTER 6

THE WARREN

The sand spit of Dawlish Warren developed about 7,000 years ago from sand and estuary deposits. After the last ice age an easterly movement of sand formed beaches in sheltered bays. The Langstone Rock and the tidal currents of the Exe estuary caused the gradual building up of the sand spit. Over the years the moving sand became trapped in plants, this resulted in the wide reaching sand dunes of today.

The first record of the Warren is to be found in the Episcopal Registers of 1280 where it is known as 'Warren in Manerio Douelis', although at some time it may have been part of the Manor of Kenton. It was, as its name suggests, a hunting ground for small game and consisted of great hills of sand, stretching further to the south east than it does today.

In the 16th century a fort was built on the far eastern tip of the Warren to control the shipping entering the River Exe. It is thought that this fort was built on the site of a much earlier one that had been built by the Saxons to give warning of approaching Danes. In this later period the ships would anchor in the deep water to the east of the Warren until the tide was full enough for them to continue up the Exe. As sand shifts with the movement of the water the anchorage was rarely in the same place twice running.

The shifting sands were ideal for one of the lucrative occupations of that time — wrecking. This was so common that it became dangerous to go out at night with a lantern as a law had been passed making it illegal to have a lantern or make a light in order to cause a shipwreck — even if no such wreck occurred. If a ship was already wrecked it was fair game for seizing and plundering as long as 'no man or cat was left alive thereon'. This signed the death warrant for both men and cats.

1782 saw a bloody naval battle between the English vessel *Defiance* and a Dutch sloop at Orcombe Point when many sailors were killed in action. Their bodies were buried in the fort area and it is said that their ghosts still haunt the sandbanks round about. Those who venture along the Warren sands on a dark and misty night may still sense an invisible, ghostly presence.

The Warren was described by the Rev. Richard Polwhele in *The History of Devonshire* (1793) as 'being in the District of Week', and, quoting

Leland, an earlier source, 'Their lyith a great waste plain and barren field to the West side and very point of Exmouth Haven. And in the West part of this haven's mouth a little above the sand goith in a Creeke, a mile or thereabout into the land. Some call it Kenton Creeke'.

The Rev. Mr Polwhele continues, 'there is a good inn at Mount Pleasant, where genteel company are frequently accommodated and there are several cottages on picturesque spots scattered around it. At the shed of this mount, we look down from the perpendicular rock on a sandy plain — over which the eye is carried to bold projections in the Cliffs and to Fissures, that at a distance seem to let in the sea, which we behold through these apertures.'

One of the cottages mentioned by Mr Polwhele was probably up beyond the Mount Pleasant Inn; this cottage became known as Langstone Cliff House and was built in the late 1700s.

As a fairly isolated and remote area the Warren ran true to form and became a notorious smugglers' haunt. The smugglers are believed to have stored their haul in the area of the Mount Pleasant Inn. Not only was there smuggling but also violent death. In 1803 a member of a naval press gang was murdered and the reputation of the Warren as a wild and lawless place was further enhanced. Physically the Warren was dramatically different from now. There was a steep bluff, about 7.5 metres high, on the seaward side of the Warren but this was washed away by a violent storm in 1859.

During the 19th century the Warren became a hive of industry. There was a salt works, which had been in operation for some time and in 1867 oyster farming was begun.

In 1862 permission was granted for the Earl of Devon to build an embankment from the southwest corner of the Exe estuary to Warren Point. The plan was to reclaim the land from the sea for oyster beds. However the Earl changed his plans and instead he built a damn and made an 80 acre lake behind the sand dunes. This is known as Greenland Lake and produced 28,000 oysters in 1867. But yet another violent storm changed the landscape and the oysters were buried under tons of sand. The end of the Earl's dream was marked by a bridge which went across the end of the lake, being called locally the Bridge of Sighs.

At the end of the 19th century, in 1891, a golf course of a few holes opened on the ideal land provided by nature and the beginning of the 20th century heralded the development of the Warren as we know it today. In 1900 the salt works were closed and holiday bungalows began to appear on the flat land. Some of these were one-roomed shacks which were added to, room by room, over the ensuing years.

Cock'ood & The Warren

The Langstone Rock, ca 1921.

A more recent view looking towards the Langstone Rock.

The large flat expanse of the Warren was ideal for gunnery target practice and in 1904 or 5, just after the Boer War, the First Rifle Volunteers used the area for just that purpose. In 1905 a railway halt was built and also, during this first decade of the 20th century, there was a hospital boat off shore. This was not strictly for use as a hospital but if, when inspected by the Health and Port Authorities, any members of the crew on an incoming ship were found to have an infectious disease, they were quarantined on this boat until their own vessel collected them on its way back to sea.

Some more building then began at the Warren. The golf course had grown and in 1910 a clubhouse was built. A new station, built on the present station site, replaced the railway halt in 1912. Unfortunately it burned to the ground almost immediately.

The nineteen twenties saw more bungalows being built on the Warren. Some of these were on stilts to keep them above any unusually high tides. They were not as simple as the earlier one-roomed shacks, some having verandahs all round. They were mostly used as holiday and weekend homes for the businessmen of Exeter. The station was also rebuilt during this period — in 1924.

Every year the sea washed away more of the Warren sands but in 1934 or 5 the spring tides and gales were to slice away great chunks of the sand dunes. The sea washed through the dunes in places and flooded the flat land behind. The water was deep enough for people to row from Exmouth to the Warren station. To round off their unusual day they could then stroll up the hill to the Mount Pleasant Inn (as described by the Rev. Richard Polwhele in 1793). By 1939 most of the bungalows at the farther end of the Warren had been destroyed.

With the threat of war looming the War Office requisitioned the remaining properties and declared the Warren itself a no go area. An anti-aircraft gun was put in place and barbed wire entanglements appeared along the beaches.

After the end of the war, in 1945/6, the defences were cleared away. The houses were gradually cleaned, redecorated and restored to their owners and day huts were erected along the shore. These latter, however, frequently disappeared with the winter storms.

The bungalows, nestling in the lupin covered sand dunes and surrounded by sea and river on three sides, seemed an idyllic place to live. They were almost a mile from the road and could be reached only by walking along the beach or by a footpath across the golf course.

Cock'ood & The Warren

Warren Point in the 1930s. The aerial view shows the extreme end of the Warren at the height of its development. Some of the houses were used only as summer bungalows, but others were lived in continuously. At this time the point (within hailing distance of the Exmouth shore, with a ferry service) formed a solid Island, but all was washed away within the next thirty years.

The Warren

Cullompton Boys Brigade camp at the Warren, ca 1927.

Summer houses at the Warren, ca 1926.

Cock'ood & The Warren

The Warren

A series of views of the Mount Pleasant Inn. Bottom left shows the fire of 1956. Top right shows the view from what is now the car park with Granny Tarr's cottage in the foreground. Bottom right shows a similar view some time after the cottage has disappeared, seemingly replaced by a small tent!

Cock'ood & The Warren

Side and front views of The Langstone Cliff Hotel, ca 1947.

The Warren

Recent photograph of The Welcome Inn. This was once a gentleman's residence known as Warren House. It had beautiful landscaped grounds containing a magnificent Tulip tree. These grounds stretched as far as the present Post Office. A coachmans house and stables stood next to the house and there was a lodge on the corner where the Golden Acre flats are now situated.

The Round House at Dawlish Warren in August 1937. It was one of a number of permanent homes which used to stand next to the beach.

67

Idyllic surroundings they may have been but not a very easy way of life. By the 1940s most houses had electricity and/or mains gas, but not these bungalows. Aladdin and Tilley lamps and oil cookers were as modern as they got. Then there was the problem of living on sand dunes. Sand got everywhere and so floors had to be swept frequently. Being so close to the sea also meant that salt water, carried on the wind, encrusted the windows, which made frequent cleaning essential. Although there was a small local shop near the station some essentials could only be obtained by taking a three-mile bike ride into Dawlish or by boat over to Exmouth.

Changes were in store for Langstone Cliff House (built in the 1700s and mentioned earlier). This had become one of the larger houses in the area and in 1946 it was bought by Stanley and Marjorie Rogers and opened as the Langstone Cliff Hotel in 1947. From the outset this was a family run, quality hotel. Over the years it has grown in size and reputation. In 1997 the hotel marked its 50th anniversary and is still very much a family concern.

The outside world brought one of its worse aspects to the Warren in the mid-fifties when the day huts and few remaining bungalows were attacked by vandals. Buildings were broken into and property stolen. There was destruction and mess everywhere.

That destruction, however, was not so great as the destruction of 1962. A tremendous storm in March swept away the remaining bungalows leaving the area almost without a trace of their existence. There had been many schemes tried since 1946 to halt the erosion but none was able to withstand the force of nature at its most powerful.

In 1970 the Devon River Board spent £340,000 to stabilise the dune. They planted marram grass which, with the lupins, serve to hold the sand in place. Along the sea side concrete has been poured to bank up the dunes, sloping down to the beach and the sea like the side of a shallow bowl so that, unless the tide is very high, the sea does not wash over on to the land.

Behind the beach the Warren has developed into a popular tourist area with cafes, shops, amusement arcades and an amusement park. Large car parks cover the flat areas that once were flooded and caravan sites and holiday flats dominate the surrounding area.

The golf course is still a popular attraction; having been described as one of the best in the country. The course is now owned by the Devon Trust for Nature Conservation who play a large part in the life of the Warren as it is today, as, beyond the golf course, there is a nature conservation area where there have been many sightings of birds, rare to this part of the world, and some unusual, and endangered plants grow.

CHAPTER 7

THE WAR YEARS

With the outbreak of the Second World War defensive measures were undertaken to try to prevent invasion. Along the promenade at Dawlish Warren huge rolls of barbed wire were erected. Large crossed metal stanchions were installed at the mouth of the River Exe. Pill boxes were built; one still remains on the edge of the golf course. A minefield was laid on the Warren adjacent to the golf course and this had one tragic consequence. A young Naval officer playing a round of golf attempted to retrieve his ball which had gone over the fence marking the boundary of the minefield. Unfortunately he set off one of the mines and was killed.

Other aspects of the defences included a look out post on the high ground alongside Lady's Mile walk and a searchlight battery was located in the woods above Eastdon House. In addition there was a gun position on the high ground above Kenbury Crescent. Soldiers were billeted in the area, notably in two semi-detached houses at the bottom of Shutterton Lane and in the old Forte's tea shop on the Warren.

In common with most country areas, evacuees came from towns and cities and were allocated to various families, although not elderly folk. Air Raid Precaution Wardens were appointed and with great officiousness insisted on every smallest glimmer of light being extinguished. In due course Home Guard platoons were formed and took part in sentry duties, although with the most pathetic array of "arms" initially.

There was considerable enemy aircraft activity above and around the estuary. It seems likely that this was a possible navigational checkpoint for bombers before they set course to bomb inland targets. At the time of the Exeter blitz many of the bombers made their way up the Exe to approach their target. Bombs were dropped in the Dawlish Warren area, including a clutch of four 1000-lb bombs. Two of these dropped in the soft marshy grounds near Shutterton Brook and did not explode. As far as is known they are still there for they were never dealt with by a bomb disposal squad.

Enemy aircraft came in very low to get under the radar defences. They tended to fire on anything that moved and it is not surprising that trains

Cock'ood & The Warren

running along the coastal line were attacked. In fact three were hit and a local resident who lived at the Warren throughout the war recalls the sound of steam escaping from the boilers of one train long after the attack.

Local residents were not supposed to go on to the beaches but some mothers managed to cut the barbed wire and crawl through with their children. But again it was necessary to be alert for incoming enemy aircraft. If one or more was spotted the drill was to grab a child and rush into the water before any attack could come, thereby lessening the risk of injury, particularly through cannon shell splinters ricocheting off the rocks.

On one occasion residents followed with interest the sight of aerial combat above the Warren. Eventually one of the aircraft was hit and lost height, finally crashing on Woodbury Common. The spectators cheered at what they assumed was the destruction of an enemy aircraft. Unfortunately it later transpired that the crashed aircraft was one of our own with several VIPs on board. It had not obtained clearance to fly into the area before leaving Plymouth and had been attacked by one of our fighters.

Another occurrence which caused a lot of interest was on January 27th, 1943 when a U.S. Army B17 (Flying Fortress) bomber was seen circling the area, clearly looking for a suitable open space to make a forced landing. From the 303rd Bomber group, the plane had lost two engines through flak over Brest. A third engine failed over the Devon coast and, after ordering

The U.S. Army B17 (Flying Fortress) bomber after its' forced landing in the grounds of Langdon Hospital, January 1943.

The War Years

his crew to bail out, Lieutenant George Oxrider landed his aircraft in a field at Langdon Hospital. After the aircraft had had three new engines fitted a temporary runway was created in the hospital grounds and the aircraft was able to take off and return to base. Lt Oxrider was decorated for his bravery but was killed in a later operation.

There was an interesting sequel some 50 years later. The wireless operator/air gunner, who had bailed out and landed at Gidleigh on Dartmoor and had become a pastor on his return to the U.S.A. made a sentimental return to Gidleigh and Dawlish in January 1993. One resident who had witnessed the landing was able to meet this crewmember and exchange memories of the event.

The forces of nature continued to play their part in shaping events. A coal boat went aground on the Pole Sands and its back was broken. It was towed originally to a point near Starcross and later to the bight, where the remains of the vessel are still visible. As the boat started breaking up its cargo of coal began to be washed up on the beaches. For the local people it was a heaven-sent opportunity to gather this coal to supplement the fuel ration which they received from normal sources.

At one time there were some 50 bungalows on the Warren, many of them strongly built and well equipped. They provided excellent accommodation for their owners. However, early in the war a ferocious southeasterly gale coincided with a spring tide and a large part of the Warren was washed away, taking with it half of the bungalows. Again nature had produced a benefit for the local people, as driftwood from the smashed bungalows was washed up on many of the local beaches, from where it could be gathered for firewood. Later another southeasterly gale caused a further 23 holiday homes to be swept away. One of the remaining two was later dismantled but the last one served as a home for some years after the war until it, too, was swept away in a gale.

It might be thought that shopping would have been very difficult during the war years, with limited public transport and most people having a bicycle as their only personal transport. However, those living in the Warren were well served with deliveries of food to the door. Two milkmen, one being Mr Nicholls of Eastdon Farm, delivered daily, three bakers called each week and a greengrocer called once a week. If a joint of meat was required then an early telephone call to the butcher would result in his errand boy delivering the order by 11 am.

Of course, most people attempted to grow as many vegetables as possible in their gardens and many kept chickens and ducks; thus

The wreck of the South Coaster, ca 1942.

The wreck as it can be seen today. Little coal left to be found and a haven for cormorants at high tide.

supplementing the meagre wartime rations. Living near the coast meant that there was opportunity to gather the harvest from the sea. On spring tides fishing for Bass was nearly always successful and lobsters could be caught amongst the rocks near Langstone Rock. One local family succeeded in catching about 100 lobsters per year in this way.

As the time of the invasion of Europe drew near, U.S. forces appeared in the area, some practising the use of D.U.K.W. amphibious vehicles in landing on enemy-held shores, with the sand dunes at the Warren serving as a practice area. One day a mother was walking with her 4 year old son along the promenade when an American serviceman hailed them and asked if the boy would like to ride in the D.U.K.W. Naturally the boy accepted the offer eagerly and he and his mother climbed into the vessel. It manoeuvred down the dunes and into the sea. After a while another D.U.K.W. came alongside and the driver of the first asked the boy if he would like to drive. What 4 year old boy could resist such an offer, So the driver engaged in lowest gear, handed over to the boy and then transferred to the second vessel, leaving the boy to cruise slowly around the area off the Dawlish Warren beach. What an example of the informality and kindness of many of the U.S. servicemen.

One day the Exe estuary was suddenly seen to be full of barges moored alongside one another across the full width of the estuary. There was much speculation as to the purpose for which these barges were intended. Then a few days later they had all disappeared. It was learnt later that these had been pontoons which formed part of the Mulberry Harbour which was set up on the French coast as part of the invasion equipment.

CHAPTER 8

CLUBS & SOCIETIES

Dawlish Warren Golf Club

The Dawlish Warren Golf Club was founded in 1892. Originally the course was of nine holes laid out on a spit of land amounting to some 85 acres. The first President was the Earl of Devon and the first secretary was the Rev. Charles Benthall, vicar of Cofton. Sunday play was not permitted until well into the twentieth century.

The annual subscription was one guinea and there were 41 members when the club started. The course record for two rounds was 86, held by the professional and visitors were allowed to play free for three days; thereafter the charges were five shillings a fortnight and ten shillings a month.

The present clubhouse was built on its existing site in 1906 and the previous one turned into the professional's hut which now stands alongside the first tee. The sea had caused the first clubhouse to be abandoned. Today's clubhouse was extensively modernised in the 1980s.

Of the early professionals no man did more to put the club on the map of Devon golf than Joe Chitty. He learned his golf at Littlehampton where he was much influenced by Rowland Jones, the English International. He joined the Warren in 1905 where he remained until his retirement in 1947 — a period only interrupted by service in the First World War as a guardsmen in the Kings Company of Grenadier Guards. He is remembered as a fine teacher of the game "an absolute gentleman who was a great stickler for the rules and etiquette of the game".

The course was extended to a full eighteen holes in 1904 with five holes on the inland side of the railway line. A lease on generous terms granted to the club by the Earl of Devon made it possible to reconstruct the course entirely within the peninsula. New holes were created on ground reclaimed from the waters of the Exe. By 1927 the lay out pretty well assumed its present form, although there have been changes as storms and tide continued to govern the overall shape of the Warren.

Conservation of the peninsula and the golf course has meant a

Clubs & Societies

The original Warren Golf Club Hut. Note the "Bridge of Sighs" in the background (see p. 59).

continuing battle against the elements on both the seaward and river borders over the years. During the first half of the century the far end of the Warren contained a village of wooden bungalows, some on stilts and some built to a very high specification. These were washed away by storms in 1946 and the early fifties and the succeeding erosion swallowed up the lovely ninth hole out on the point of the course. During the early seventies various revisions to the course plan had to be made to compensate for the loss of yardage in that area and eventually the present format evolved.

In 1974 there was a further breach, this time of the river defences on the inland side of the course which completely flooded the back nine from the seventeenth green to the seventh fairway Much work has since been undertaken by the authorities. Sea defences are now a great deal more secure, Although aerial photographs illustrate vividly the overall vulnerability of the Warren at the mouth of a strong tidal estuary.

During the Second World War the army took over the club. They constructed defences on the beach and gun emplacements on the course. A line of land mines was laid from the 17th green across to the 2nd fairway, behind what is now the 10th green. This area was covered with barbed wire leaving a safe way through to play the foreshortened 2nd hole and the rest of the course. Further out on the right of the 6th an area was used for aircraft practising cannon fire. Despite this, golf continued to be played on a somewhat modified course, though players were forbidden to fetch golf balls from the mined area.

The clubhouse was requisitioned. All but two bedrooms and the kitchen were taken over by the Army and the secretary moved into the ladies trolley shed. Thankfully the defences were never put to the test and after the war life slowly returned to normal. The land and buildings were derequisitioned and compensation of £1,250 was received.

In 1961 Colonel and Mrs Creasy purchased the course from the Earl of Devon. It is recorded in the club committee minutes of June 30th 1960 that the offer of Colonel and Mrs Creasy to purchase depended on the specific understanding that there would always be a golf course on the land in question, or the land should be vested in the National Trust or similar organisations. In 1976, however, ownership of the course passed by gift from the Creasy family to the Devon Trust for Nature Conservation, now renamed The Devon Wildlife Trust. The course is leased to the club for a peppercorn rent. For the named trustees represent the clubs interests in this amicable arrangement.

Today there are more than 550 members, the majority of whom are playing members. The game is enjoying a great boom of popularity, much as it must have done over a century ago when the Rev. Charles Benthall and his wife started to knock a ball about the Warren and so conceived the idea of founding a club there. As heirs of proud tradition today's members will do everything possible to ensure that the future generations will be able to continue to enjoy the game of golf in this beautiful setting.

Whist Drive

About 70 years ago several locals decided to set up a Whist Drive, Lionel Dodge being just one of the driving forces. It was started up as a family "association" at a cost of 9 d a ticket. The Whist Drive still continues today under the leadership of Kath Bloomfield and meets regularly in the parish room. It has contributed greatly to the parish room over the years, and the current tables and curtains are courtesy of this organisation.

Cofton Women's Institute

The Institute was formed in October 1938 with 36 members present at the first meeting. It has continued to the present day. For some years after WW2 there was a separate Institute at Dawlish Warren but this closed in 1972. Cockwood and District Institute started in 1979 but closed in 1982.

Cofton Institute had scarcely become established before WW2 began. Thereafter the records show a wide range of activities that were typical of the wartime years: knitting garments for people serving in the forces; raising money for the Spitfire Fund and the WI ambulance; donations to the Plymouth distress fund, Exeter Air Raid Distress fund, the Red Cross and many other causes.

Attendance at monthly meetings was often poor, which was not surprising in view of the many other demands upon people's time and energies. One of these involving WI members was the setting up and running of a preserving centre, using fruit available in the area.

This was a well-organised and supervised scheme, with Ministry of Food inspectors assessing the quality of the produce. It was a large operation with the Cofton centre producing 1360 lb of jam in 1941 and 1652 lb of jam and 76 lb of chutney in 1942. In all, the Centre produced 5296 lb of

Tree planting by members of the Cofton WI.

Members of the Cofton WI working at St Mary's Church Hall, Dawlish Warren.

jam and 210 lb of chutney through the efforts of these voluntary workers.

The coming of peace saw the Institute develop a more normal pattern of activities. However, concern was still felt for those who had suffered as a result of the war and in 1955 it was decided to adopt a family of refugees. The adults had been brought from the Ukraine to Germany as slave labour during the war and were living in a refugee camp at the time of the adoption.

Over the next 15 years Cofton WI gave material to support this family by way of presents, clothes, food parcels and money. In April 1963 the daughter attended the monthly meeting to express the thanks of the family for the help they had received.

The Institute was active in making donations to a number of causes, including a contribution to the Devon Federation fund to purchase a coastal area at Little Dartmouth. This was presented to the National Trust and forms part of the South Devon Coastal Footpath. Nearer home, the Institute made a number of donations to help the parish room in the purchase of Stage Curtains, three large tables and a water heater. To mark the millennium the Institute donated cushions for the chairs in the parish room.

After 60 years membership still stands at over 30 with meetings held regularly in the parish room and with the Institute looking forward with confidence to the new millennium.

Mothers' Union

The Cofton branch of the Mothers' Union was formed in 1952, largely as a result of the enthusiasm and drive of the late Mrs May Chivers. She became the first enrolling member and, under her leadership, the branch grew rapidly.

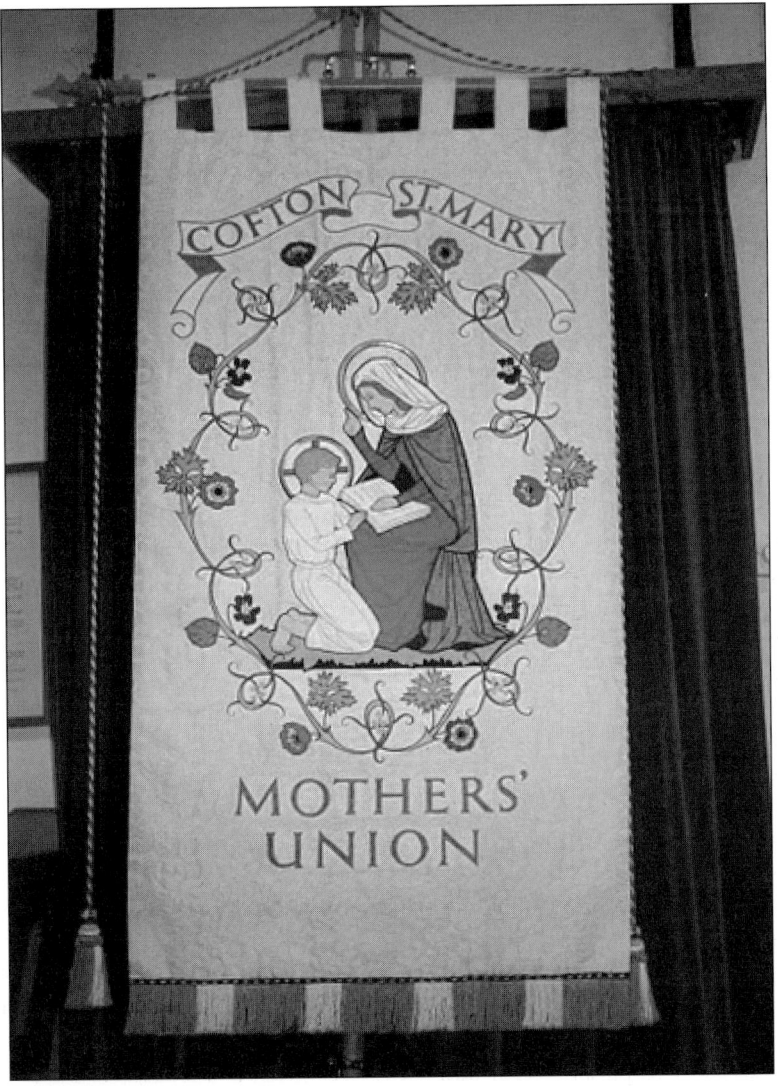

Mothers' Union banner dedicated in 1955. On display in St Mary's Church.

Spurred on by her enthusiasm, money was raised for the M.U. banner which is now in St Mary's Church. It was her idea that the border of the banner should depict the local flowers that grow here: violets, anemones, and the Warren crocus. These are arranged as a border to the centre of the banner which depicts the Virgin Mary instructing the child Jesus. The banner was made by Wippels of Exeter and was dedicated in 1955.

In the 1980s Cofton and Starcross branches were combined and now meet regularly in St Paul's Church, Starcross.

Cockwood Boat Club

By the middle of the 1960s Dr Beeching, the then Transport Minister, was wielding his axe on the rail network. Rumours abounded on the future of the rail link south of Exeter. If this link was severed it seemed likely that the three tunnels under the railway bridges affording access to Cockwood Harbour (for some time known as the Sod) would be dismantled and replaced by large drainage pipes. This would have ended centuries of boat access to and from the River Exe. At this time the central tunnel was filled in by British Rail with an accompanying threat to effect further economies by filling in the arch under the Iron Bridge. Fears, fed by rumour, led to talk of plans to construct a road across the Sod, inside the would-be disused railway line, thereby by-passing Cockwood Bridge. Certainly distinct warning bells were ringing.

On January 15th 1968 a small group of pioneers called a public meeting at Cockwood and formed a "Cockwood and District Boating Association". The declared aim being to "promote the interest of boat owners who moored their boats in Cockwood Harbour". The annual subscription was fixed at one shilling per year (5 p). A Mr J. S. Reeves was appointed Chairman and a Mr P. Brazell honorary secretary. A founder member, Mr John Newberry, one of the four original trustees, still holds office as the Honorary Harbour Bosun.

The growing popularity of water-based activities necessitated a further step in order to establish a more effective control over moorings. Later the same year negotiations were started with the Crown Estate Commissioners, the owners of the harbour, for the purpose of obtaining a lease. In order to do so it was necessary to establish a non-statutory body to be known as the Cockwood Sod Fairways Committee.

During 1973 support was obtained in principle for the proposal from the relevant authorities and this was followed by a crowded public meeting in the parish room chaired by the then secretary Tim Saunders. The case for the control of moorings was presented by Colonel Oliver R. Jackson (shortly to become President of the organisation). Unanimous approval was given to the obtaining of a lease and for the designation of the Cockwood Sod as a conservation area. The lease from the Crown was finally obtained in March 1974 with the conservation area status being achieved the following year.

Under the terms of the lease the Cockwood Sod Fairways Committee has a duty to "preserve the beauties and safeguard the ancient usage and amenities of the Cockwood Sod". This provides facilities for boat users, bird watchers and artists alike to enjoy a natural harbour — a rare thing these days.

The Cockwood Boat Club has grown in strength over the years. It is essentially a non-profit organisation and arguably provides the cheapest moorings anywhere in the country.

Cockwood Monday Club

The club was founded in 1982 with the object of supplying a focal point for the village where lady members could meet and socialise, have fun and raise money for local charities.

Monday Club members with one of their many prize winning Carnival floats.

Cock'ood & The Warren

The club meets regularly on the third Monday of each month in the parish room and the meeting usually welcomes a guest speaker, often with local connections, who gives a talk on interesting subjects such as a beautician, a fortune teller, flower arranging and birds of prey.

Regular activities include Bingo and Jumble Sales, Day Trips, Mystery Trips, Fashion Shows and visits to the Theatre. The club enters the Dawlish Carnival each year and arranges a Christmas Meal at a local hostelry and in the past has put on shows in the parish room. There are currently over 60 members and the club welcomes ladies of all ages living within the area.

Mother & Toddler Group

The group was started in 1988 with four or five local mothers and their children and has grown steadily to its present size, where an average of ten families attend each week. Its aim is to provide an opportunity for parents to meet and make friends, and for their children to develop their social skills through play and interaction with others.

The group meets every Monday afternoon, except Bank Holidays, at the Cofton Parish Room, and is open to parents with their pre-school children from all surrounding areas. Besides all the regular meetings where the children are able to make use of the large variety of toys provided, periodic outings, toy, clothes and book parties and special events, such as a Christmas Party, are arranged.

Most of the money required to pay for the hire of the hall, and to replenish the stock of toys comes from subscriptions paid weekly by the parents who attend. The subscription also covers refreshment during the afternoon.

The group is run on a voluntary basis and relies on the co-operation of all those who attend in helping to set up and put away equipment, making the drinks and washing up, and to support fund raising activities.

Cockwood Cockleshell Mariners

Sometime in April 1997 a group of local people were discussing the various clubs in the Village and it was discovered that there was not a club that was purely a Social Club for men, women and children. These same people met again and this time agreed that there was an opening for a club in the Village to arrange social events whether they are in the village or trips away. A public meeting was held in the parish room and attended by quite a number of people who were interested in joining such a club.

The children of Cockwood School were given the task of suggesting a name for this new Village Club. After going through all the suggested names, a vote was taken and the Cockwood Cockleshell Mariners was the winner. And so a new club was formed. The membership started at about 20 but now has risen to approximately 80.

It is basically a fun club designed for all of the family and as such the officers were named Cob, Pen, Cygnet 1 and Cygnet 2, in addition to the Secretary and Treasurer of course! Some of the many popular events that have been held are: Day at the Races at Newton Abbot, Boat trips, assorted theme evenings at local Greek, Italian and Spanish restaurants and a Dartmouth steam train trip.

Cofton in Bloom

Cofton in Bloom embraces the parish of Cofton, bounded by Mount Pleasant Road, Dawlish Warren Road and Exeter Road between Dawlish and Cockwood. Competitions have been held annually for the best displays of hanging baskets and tubs, and for best kept gardens since 1995, the idea inspired and organised by Mrs Joyce Anthony. Shields, trophies and cups have been and still are awarded to the winners.

In 1997 the "inspiration" was formed into a club with a Constitution and Rules the primary objects being to encourage members to participate in growing plants and flowers to beautify their gardens and therefore the villages of Cofton in general. With their experience of "Usk in Bloom" Mr and Mrs Geoffrey Drought introduced the idea of general floral decoration throughout the parish, particularly around the Harbour at Cockwood.

Since 1997, membership has blossomed to about a third of the population of Eastdon, Westwood, Middlewood and Cockwood. With member's participation in watering and tending the hanging baskets and troughs that adorn St Mary's Church, Cockwood Harbour and elsewhere during the summer months, functions are held for fund raising, local and social benefit. In 1999, The club was entered in the National "Small villages in Bloom" competition for the first time, the results of which proved that we are still on a learning curve!

A Short Story. Fact or Fiction ?

The Warren seemed to be totally silent except for the slight stir of the wind from off the sea. Clouds almost covered the moon that appeared occasionally and showed a calm sea lapping gentle onto the shore. The tide was almost high and at its highest for the month.

Approaching the shore the French clipper moved almost with complete silence. Heading straight in towards the shore it appeared quite ghostly in appearance with only one sail needed to keep it coming ahead. About two hundred yards from the shore the boat came around and the sail dropped as if without any command. Making no noise at all two sailors ran to the bow of the clipper and lifted a large weight anchor over the side. Quietly they dropped the weight into the sea on a strong rope. No chains were used as this would be heard a long way off. The weight sunk to the bottom and the clipper came to a halt and gently swung into the wind. Well-greased davits swung a rowing boat over the side. Three men entered the boat, three kegs of brandy and two large bundles of silk were loaded and then quietly the boat was lowered to the sea. Two of the men placed the oars in well-muffled rowlocks and began with strong strokes to pull towards the shore.

About 50 yards from the shore the third member in the boat gave a signal and the crewmen stopped rowing. They sat in the gentle swell and craned their eyes on the shore. After what seemed to be a long time a light flashed and then went out only to be repeated three times and then came on and stayed on. The signal was for the coast to be clear and they could land safely. The oarsmen pulled hard towards the shore and soon they felt the sandy bottom grate against the boat and they came to a standstill. The third member of the crew who seemed to be in charge jumped into the water and waded the few yards to the shore. His hand rested on a loaded flintlock pushed into his waistband. His nerves were on edge as he waited to see who would approach their landing place.

Four men moved quickly down from the dunes, one carrying the lantern that had been used to give the signal. Greetings were passed between the group in French and the tension in the air seemed to ease. The man with the lamp produced a small leather pouch and handed it to the Frenchman.

As he did so the chink of coins or gold could be heard, a whispered 'merci' was uttered as he signalled his crewmen to unload the cargo. Each of the Englishmen took a keg and the man with the lamp took the two bundles. Giving the boat a hefty push the Frenchman, happy to be leaving so quickly, again entered the water and then jumped into the boat. The oarsmen rapidly pulled away and headed back to the clipper. The Englishmen ran swiftly towards the dunes with their cargo using as much cover as they could so as not to be seen out in the open if the moon should appear from behind the clouds.

Once they reached the cover of the dunes they stopped and lay still and listened. The Coastguard and Custom Officers in this area were known to be out at night and they frequently used horses to move around the coast quickly, arriving when least expected. The night was still and nothing could be heard, each of the men felt quite elated. Once again they had managed to beat the Customs Officers and each would earn themselves a good reward for the part they had played in bringing in the contraband. As they peered seaward they could just see in the far distance the French clipper disappearing. It had made good headway after the crewmembers had returned from the shore.

With nothing stirring the Englishmen started to move along the dunes gaining confidence with each step. After about twenty minutes of running through the soft sand dunes and grass they reached the bottom of the steep hill leading to the top of the cliff. This was the final hurdle to safety. All they needed to do was to get to the top of the hill, go to the back of the Inn and await the Landlord who was expecting them. By now they were feeling slightly tired as the tension was beginning to take its toll.

They waited for a few minutes to regain their breath, with a nod the man with the lamp moved ahead leading the way up the track to the back of the Inn. Parts of the track were quite difficult to cover as the track had been worn into the side of the cliff by walkers making their way down to the waters edge. They arrived at the point about forty yards from the Inn and stopped partly concealed by an outcrop of rocks. Now they would have to wait for the signal from the landlord that the coast was all clear.

Meanwhile in the Inn the Landlord was standing in what appeared to be an almost asleep pose, next to his bar. The evening had been quite a quiet one with fewer customers than usual. Although he wasn't surprised as the weather had seemed quite threatening and this always meant a quiet time. No one wished to walk back through the fields on a wet night. The bar had only five customers in total. Four were regulars who always took all evening

Cock'ood & The Warren

to drink just two pints of beer. The fifth customer was an older man who always seemed to be smoking his pipe and gave his name as Jim. He had arrived two weeks ago and was staying in the Inn's best room. Jim had a large dog and each morning he left the Inn at about ten o'clock with the dog. Jim told the landlord that he was on a visit to the area with a view to purchasing a farm in Devon and was very surprised how many were for sale. Not having a horse to get around it was taking him a lot of time to cover the area.

Every so often the landlord seemed to rouse from his slumber and look at his watch. At about ten thirty he disappeared into the back of the Inn and was gone for about ten minutes. Outside the men waiting behind the rocks were starting to feel rather agitated when the rear door of the Inn opened and a light shone out very brightly. Almost immediately the door closed again. The door reopened and closed again. This happened four times, the signal that the coast was clear. The men dashed forward with their contraband and into the Inn. The Landlord showed them quickly into the cellar and a very dark corner where they placed the kegs and bundles. 'Well done' was heard and 'call tomorrow'. The men left with high hopes.

The Landlord returned to the bar only to see that no one had stirred whilst he was away. Happily he returned to his sleepy pose, but this time behind the bar. In his mind he was calculating how much profit this evening had made after he had paid his men.

Jim who had had a long day rose to his feet, paused looking out of the window, struck a match and once again lit his pipe. The only difference this time was that it seemed to take a little longer than usual for the tobacco to light. He walked over to the bar next to the Landlord. He placed a small wallet on the bar and then said 'by my calculation you owe me one pound eighteen shillings three pence and three farthings. But by all means correct me if I am wrong'. With this he opened the wallet to show the Landlord the insignia of a crown on a background of water. The dreaded crest of Customs Officers.

The Landlord, rather taken back, moved slightly to his left and reached down behind the bar where he always kept a loaded flintlock pistol. He was about to produce it and 'deal with' the Customs Officer. He knew that there was no love between the locals and the law and whatever action he took would only cost him a few pints over the next week or two, when the front door and the rear door behind him opened and two uniformed militia, with cocked muskets, entered at each. Slowly he stood up straight reached into his trouser pocket and produced a leather string drawn purse. Grudgingly he said 'I trust you have change for two guineas'.

86

Acknowledgements

As with all publications of this type there are an enormous number of people and organisations to thank for a variety of reasons. The restrictions of space and accuracy of memory make it impossible to name all of them individually but I hope that those individuals not mentioned here will gain some pleasure from seeing their contribution in print.

A special debt of gratitude is acknowledged to Peter Kay for allowing the use of extracts and photographs from his book *Exeter to Newton Abbot: A Railway History*, which gives a detailed account of the development of that section of the railway system. In addition, Basil Macer-Wright is thanked for permitting extracts of his book *Living by the Ninth Green* to be used in the chapter on Dawlish Warren. The summary of the Dawlish Warren Golf Club is included by kind permission of Douglas Peterkin, former club President, from whose book *The Story of the Warren Golf Club* it unashamedly borrows. Mr A. C. Hopkins is thanked for the photograph of the clubhouse.

Official sources and local organisations, and their staff are thanked as follows:

Cockwood Primary School
Dawlish Museum
Devon Records Office
Starcross Fishing & Cruising Club
The Anchor Inn
The Langstone Cliff Hotel
WestCountry Studies Library

Dawlish Library
Dawlish Newspapers Ltd
The Earl of Devon
St Mary's Church, Cofton
The Ship Inn
The Mount Pleasant Inn

For financial support thanks are due to the Community Council of Devon, Rural Initiatives Loan Fund and the Cofton Millennium Committee. Special thanks are also due to Mr W. G. Jeffery.

The authors are applauded for their tremendous efforts and the representatives of the Clubs & Societies mentioned in the book are thanked for their time and input. A personal thanks to David Miller and Anita Mason at The Studio for their advice and expertise.

Last, but not least, a huge thank you to all those local villagers and friends who have either supplied pictures or text together with encouragement and support. This book has been produced for you.

Publishers Note

Comment, correspondence and further material pertaining to the history of the area covered in this book would be welcomed by the Publisher.